A Century of Railways

around Birmingham and the West Midlands
VOLUME TWO
1948 – 1972

A superb shot of Bushbury shedded "Jubilee" No.45738 "Samson" preparing to leave New Street with a Euston express, about 1955.
(Maurice Newman collection)

a personal selection by
JOHN BOYNTON

INTRODUCTION

"May you live in interesting times"
- old Chinese saying

This book consists of three chapters, each beginning with an event that was important for the railways. It opens in 1948 with the birth of British Railways. Chapter Two starts in 1955 with the publication of the Modernisation Plan. The final chapter begins with the publication of the Beeching Report in 1963 and ends with the closure of Birmingham's much loved Snow Hill station in 1972. For the sake of continuity the events described are not always placed rigidly within these chapters. Dieselisation began before 1955, but the whole progress of events is included in Chapter Two; Coventry station was rebuilt before 1963, but it is included with the other redeveloped stations in Chapter Three.

The 1950s and 60s were certainly 'interesting times' for the railways of the West Midlands. At the beginning of this period there was a final recovery from wartime conditions. Expresses once again linked Birmingham with London in two hours. New Standard steam locomotives became familiar sights in the region. Mixed traffic Class 5s were to be seen at New Street in charge of expresses on the Bristol-Derby main line and the heavy freight 9F 2-10-0s were spectacularly successful on almost any duty, freight or passenger.

The 1955 Modernisation Plan recognised that the network needed serious investment in order to thrive. This led to the widespread use of new diesel multiple units on most local services in the West Midlands by 1960. Grubby, irregular steam trains gave way to the dmus, which were cleaner, more frequent and generally ran at regular intervals. They transformed the image of local rail services. As a result many stations saw a significant increase in the number of passengers, which helped to save some lines from closure during the 1960s.

As the 50s gave way to the 60s, the increasing availability of new diesel locomotives helped build up the speed and frequency of main line services. At a time when the number of car owners was rising faster than ever before, an effective network of long distance coach services was established and new motorways were being built, it was vital that the railways continued to modernise in this way. With the May 1972 time-table changes, Birmingham New Street became the hub around which British Rail's long distance passenger network was built. Meanwhile, between 1960 and 1967, the icing on the cake was briefly provided by the Birmingham built 'Blue Pullman', an innovative diesel train which operated the business service on the Snow Hill-Paddington route, bringing a certain style to rail travel for the fortunate few.

Three of the most important stations in the region, at Coventry, Birmingham New Street and Wolverhampton High Level, were completely rebuilt as part of the electrification programme for the West Coast Main Line. Scores of old manual signalboxes, and a handful of new ones less than ten years old, were swept away as power boxes took shape at just five key locations. The huge marshalling yard at Bescot was ruthlessly grubbed up, like an old hedge, replaced by a new yard within a year. The 'new' way to handle freight, trumpeted by Dr.Beeching as though he had thought of it first, was in standardised containers on 'liner' trains. Freightliner depots, with mobile cranes spanning the tracks on tracks of their own, were built at Birmingham Lawley Street and Dudley.

The Chinese know only too well that the price of living in interesting times is the likelihood of turmoil and upheaval - the remark is not necessarily meant to be friendly. The price of progress in the 50s and 60s was the rapid loss of so much that had seemed solid and permanent. Of the major stations that were completely rebuilt only Coventry was a real success, yet improvement came less than three years before two of its important local lines were closed. Birmingham New Street had become a dingy old ruin but the power of market forces, as opposed to the needs of passengers, transformed it into a dingy modern nightmare.

Some lines and individual stations had endured a poor train service for years, often resulting from cutbacks made in the war which were not restored afterwards. Diesels came - perhaps - but the number of trains remained the same. Consequently the number of passengers was low and the value of such a line to its community was minimal, as was resistance when closure threatened. Alternatives to closure, such as improvements to the service, were not seriously considered in the Beeching era. Important towns, such as Dudley, Brierley Hill, Wednesbury, West Bromwich and Cannock, had lost all their passenger trains by 1972. Some stations remained open but were served by hardly any trains. Walsall lost five of its six passenger routes in 1964/5. Redditch, a government designated New Town with an hourly diesel service, found itself with just three trains a day; Bromsgrove had only one train in each direction. Former main lines were closed (Snow Hill-Wolverhampton) or threatened with closure. The North Warwickshire Line, which had a decent train service and an army of commuters who were prepared to resist, had a remarkable escape in 1969.

Steam declined with indecent haste after 1960, finishing in heaps of scrap when so many locomotives were almost new. The Freightliner trains were an excellent idea, but they were then seen as virtually the only idea for a modern freight railway. Small and medium-sized goods yards disappeared, as did the much valued door-to-door delivery service provided by the railway's own road vehicles. The wide variety of goods carried was quickly lost to road hauliers. The railway ceased to be a common carrier and wagonload traffic was turned away.

The electrification of the West Coast Main Line, completed in the Birmingham area in 1967, was a magnificent engineering achievement. The whole railway, from the trackbed up, had been completely rebuilt. Birmingham and London were now only 95 minutes apart and trains had to run at 100mph simply to keep time. Even this great leap forward had negative effects. There were plans to electrify the local lines from New Street to Four Oaks and Lichfield and from New Street to Walsall and Rugeley. They were abandoned in favour of electrification to Walsall only. Over twenty years later the route to Lichfield was electrified as part of the Cross City Line, but only after intense pressure on the government of the day, which agreed to it after the death of the MP for South Staffordshire caused a by-election which the government thought it might lose. The present absurd 'energy gap' between Walsall and Rugeley is another example of 1960s penny pinching which will soon have to be addressed.

A more immediate consequence of the 1967 electrification was the downgrading of the Snow Hill-Paddington route, and its northern extension to Shrewsbury and Birkenhead, plus the closure of Snow Hill and Wolverhampton Low Level as main line stations. Electrification of the New Street route meant that it was seen at the time as the only route, therefore the other one had to go. Fortunately this way of thinking is now seen for what it was - bizarre - especially since the opening of the new Snow Hill and the success of its restored link with London.

After 1967 Snow Hill station became a huge forlorn unstaffed halt, with just the occasional single unit railcar to Wolverhampton or Langley Green disturbing the eerie quiet. The weeds, like an advancing army of triffids, threatened to engulf the place. Not long before the last train departed in March 1972, a watershed had been crossed. Responsibility for local rail services had passed to the recently formed West Midlands Passenger Transport Authority (WMPTA) at the beginning of that year. The new authority, one of four set up by the 1968 Transport Act, was at first criticised for its apparent lack of interest in rail, and for its failure to save the Snow Hill service from closure. However, it did safeguard the trackbed and station site for future use and came to adopt a positive attitude to rail in general. Services were improved, trains and buses connected with each other, new stations were opened and - with the exception of Smethwick West - not a single station was closed after 1972.

I must reserve comments about these and other developments for the final volume of "A Century of Railways". Given the recent upturn in rail traffic, both passenger and freight, it seems likely that the story will have a happy ending. Regular steam working finished in the 1960s but Volume Three (1973-1999) will contain some steam, both on preserved railways and out on the main line. I have already been given permission to use one stunning main line shot, taken in 1997 and, if I were not already the author, I would buy the book for that picture alone.

John Boynton
1998

Black Five No.44812 eases through King's Norton with a mixed freight off the Camp Hill line, one winter's day about 1962.

(Peter Shoesmith)

CONTENTS

Rail Passenger Network
— 1948 – 1972 —

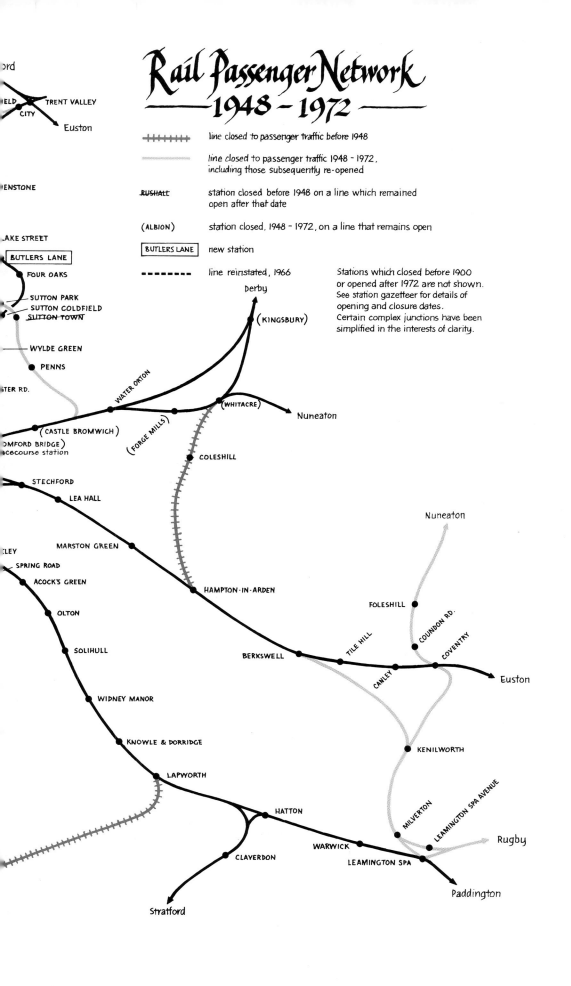

Euston

┼┼┼┼┼┼┼┼ line closed to passenger traffic before 1948

━━━━━━ line closed to passenger traffic 1948 – 1972,
including those subsequently re-opened

RUSHALL station closed before 1948 on a line which remained
open after that date

(ALBION) station closed, 1948 – 1972, on a line that remains open

BUTLERS LANE new station

- - - - - - - line reinstated, 1966

Stations which closed before 1900
or opened after 1972 are not shown.
See station gazetteer for details of
opening and closure dates.
Certain complex junctions have been
simplified in the interests of clarity.

Derby

(KINGSBURY)

CHAPTER ONE
THE UNCHANGING FACE OF THE RAILWAY, 1948-1954

[Diary : The People's Railway : A Cosmetic Exercise : Real Improvements : Shed Census, 10th March 1953]

Diary

1948

January 1st - British Railways comes into being, announced at midnight by thousands of engine whistles all over the country.

February 10th - Accident at Stourbridge Town goods, as a pannier tank loco, travelling bunker first, lost control on greasy rails down the 1:27 gradient into the goods yard. Its train of just six trucks, loaded with iron bars, was heavy enough, on such an incline, to push the loco down the grade, where it came to rest just a foot away from the goods office. Driver and fireman jumped clear, slightly injuring the latter, and the trucks formed a heap of wreckage behind the loco, scattering their contents in the process.

1949

May 23rd - Soho (ex-LMS) station closed, on the Stour Valley line, east of Smethwick Rolfe Street.

1950

July 1st - Several Black Country stations, ex-GWR and ex-LMS, were each given a suffix to distinguish between them, eg; the two Wednesbury stations became Wednesbury Central (WR) and Wednesbury Town (LMR).

October 25th - Inaugural run of a new named train, "The Midlander", Euston - Wolverhampton.

1951

October 8th - New small goods depots were still opening. Perry Barr Wharf opened on this date.

1952

Following final closure of the Whitacre to Hampton-in-Arden line, the Chester Road bridge was filled in and the road widened. Work began in January.

August 25th - Deepfields & Coseley station renamed Coseley.

1953

August 17th - New experimental diesel railcar began a week's running between Wolverhampton Low Level and Birmingham Snow Hill (see Chapter Two).

October 5th - New "Inter-City" express restores the two hour journey between Snow Hill and Paddington and unknowingly launches a new brand name.

1954

June 1st-3rd - Exhibition of rolling stock at New Street to celebrate the station's centenary. Items included Queen Adelaide's saloon coach of 1842, Queen Victoria's saloon coach of 1895, the famous LNWR 'Precedent' loco "Hardwicke" and Stanier Pacific No.46235 "City of Birmingham", which had been named at the station when new, on 20th March 1945.

September 30th - Hourly steam push-pull service introduced between New Street and Sutton Coldfield, the first real improvement to a Birmingham area local service since the Second World War, and the first to operate at regular intervals since before the First. Moor Street to Stratford and Leamington local services (still steam) also improved, with more trains and almost at regular intervals.

The People's Railway

On 1st January 1948 Britain's former railway companies - GWR, LMS, LNER, SR - became the nationalised 'British Railways', just one among a whole range of industries and utilities which passed into public ownership under Clement Attlee's Labour Government of 1945-50. The rail network was now, in the language of the time, 'owned by the people for the people'. The Transport Act of 1947, by which British Railways was brought into existence, also established a British Transport Commission (BTC) with *"the general duty to provide an efficient, adequate, economic and properly integrated system of public inland transport"*. The Commission, answerable to the Minister of Transport, would decide overall transport policy, but operation was the responsibility of five Executives - Railways, Docks & Inland Waterways, Road Transport, London Transport and Hotels (responsible for hotels formerly owned by railway companies and also for catering at stations and on trains). The BTC, wound up at the end of 1962, had not been able to provide *"an efficient, adequate, economic and properly integrated system of public transport"* during its brief life.

Today it is very clear - from the clogged state of our roads and the poor air quality in our cities - that we seem to be further away than ever from attaining such a system. Yet, so far as the railways are concerned, there have been many moves towards greater integration in the West Midlands, particularly since the 1970s.

But what was it like to work on the railway in the early years of British Railways, especially for a lad just leaving school? One such was Jim Male of Wolverhampton, who wrote, *"You will be well aware that the railway industry was always a family affair"*. He worked for over fifty years on the railway, as did his grandfather. Other members of the family also relied on the GWR for their wages. In the summer of 1946, a year into the

Attlee government, Jim left school, aged 14. (The school leaving age was not raised to 15 until 1947.) After a brief holiday he was informed by his mother, *"You are starting work on Monday at Stafford Road, I cannot keep you in idleness any longer"*.

The railway workshop was a hive of activity and Jim's first job (at 14!) was to drive one of the three steam hammers in the blacksmiths shop. In that section there were three blacksmiths, a toolsmith and a spring maker. Within the workshop there was also a large electric saw which cut red hot metal. The only women normally seen on the shop floor were the tea girls who came round twice a day, although the GWR Institute canteen was open round the clock. At lunch time Jim would go across to the erecting shop and see all the locomotives being stripped and rebuilt, *"all good stuff for a fourteen year old"*.

In October 1947 he started at Oxley shed as a cleaner, the first rung on the ladder to becoming a driver. It was enjoyable but, *"it soon became apparent what this job meant, working shifts etc. while your friends were out enjoying themselves and you were either at work or in bed."* After a few weeks he was transferred to Stafford Road shed, *"very dirty compared with Oxley, but instead of cleaning small tank engines I was now going to clean 'Kings', 'Castles' and the new 'Counties'."*

Jim was employed as a temporary fireman on the Oxley shunting engines from April 1948, and passed out in December to be a permanent fireman, at the minimum age of seventeen. He fired on local shunting and goods engines to such places as Great Bridge, Swan Village, the Wombourn line, Dudley, Netherton and Stourbridge. His career was rudely interrupted, as were so many, by two years' National Service - spent working in army cookhouses - before he returned his fireman's job in 1952. *"Considering that the railway had been nationalised in 1948 little had changed. Some of the older engines had been scrapped and*

New number, old logo. 2-6-4T No.42267 pauses at Hampton-in-Arden with a four-carriage stopping train for Coventry, 13th May 1950.
(F.W.Shuttleworth)

we acquired quite a few new ones, including some BR Standard Class 5s, 73xxx. Diesel shunters were introduced in 1953 and they could stay in service for a month. Because we were always short of firemen the loss of work was not noticed ...."

A Cosmetic Exercise

Public ownership was seen as a solution to many problems by the Attlee government, which set to work with a reforming zeal. Coal, gas, electricity, steel and water were all nationalised. January 1948 saw the formation of British Railways, followed on 5th July by the establishment of the National Health Service. The energy consumed by Parliament in passing all the necessary legislation could not be matched by similarly dramatic change and reform at ground level. The motto of the new BR could have been a nautical one, "Steady as she goes".

Many of the photographs from the period which appear in this book show the railways in a run down condition. Exhausted by super-human efforts during the war, they were denied adequate resources to aid complete recovery in the long years of austerity that followed. They were not alone in this, as the country's entire industrial base had to rely on meagre rations from a very small cake.

With small variations (see below) the former LMS lines became part of the London Midland Region and the ex-Great Western lines formed the Western Region. Differences in style soon became apparent. They attracted the enthusiast of the day, but brought little or no benefit to passengers or freight customers. Ex-LMS locos were re-numbered, the old number at first prefixed by an 'M', soon replaced by a '4'. The prefix '5' was reserved for the gereatric locos reprieved from the scrapyard by wartime necessity and still needed for menial duties. As numbers on ex-Great Western locos had never been merely painted on but always cast in relief, they were left unchanged.

BR experimented with new locomotive liveries in the early years, some of which could regularly be seen in the West Midlands, especially on the ex-Great Western lines. Some "Kings", including "King George V", were painted an alien but attractive blue between 1949 and 1951. It is sometimes forgotten now, that other Great Western classes which had always been Brunswick Green - Saints, Stars, Halls, Granges and Manors - were considered mixed traffic types by the new regime and were therefore painted black between 1948 and 1956. They were lined in red, with a signal red background for their nameplates. The Castles were never black but one, 4091 "Dudley Castle" was painted another experimental colour briefly in vogue, apple green, *and* given a brass numberplate on its smokebox in 1949.

The once familiar station name 'totems' were an early sign that British Railways was adopting its own corporate identity. Those on the London Midland Region (New Street lines) were dark red; on the Western (Snow Hill) they were chocolate brown. Such totems are now collectors' items, commanding hundreds of pounds. *(courtesy of Birmingham Post & Mail)*

Following nationalisation, locos soon began to appear with BRITISH RAILWAYS emblazoned on the tender. As a rapid sequel to this, the first type of BR lion logo (officially referred to as a 'totem') was introduced in 1949. The lion was stylish but impossibly deformed, as his anorexic body arched high above the totem's wheel. The second totem, the 'lion and wheel', showed the beast emerging from the top of a crown, wagging his tongue and grasping a wheel in his red paws. He lasted long enough to grace the sides of steam and diesel locos, plus many new Mark I coaches and dmus. A cast metal version appeared on early West Coast electric locos, which began visiting New Street in 1967.

New colour identities were established for the regions, to be used on stations, signalboxes,etc. The London Midland (LMR) used a maroon and cream scheme, while the Western (WR) continued with their version of chocolate and cream, officially described as beech brown and champagne beige. For rolling stock, non-corridor local passenger carriages were red on both regions. Ex-LMS main line carriages briefly flirted with a main line livery very similar to that of the old LNWR (see Volume One, front cover and pages 66-67) before the new carmine and cream (blood and custard) became widespread on both regions, even down to some of the ex-GW diesel railcars. It was smart but difficult to keep clean and from 1955 was superseded by overall maroon. At this the Western Region authorities, between 1956 and 1962, repainted as much express passenger stock as they could in chocolate and cream. Thus it was briefly possible, at the end of the 1950s, to stand at the top of the steps to Platform 7 at Birmingham Snow Hill, watch the arrival of the 9am to Paddington behind a "King" and wonder indeed whether this was 1959 or 1939.

Several places in the Black Country had two stations, both with the same name, often reflecting the rivalries of old companies which refused to acknowledge each other's existence. With effect from 1st july 1950 the situation was clarified. The two Wednesbury stations became Central (WR) and Wednesbury Town (LMR); The Tiptons became Tipton Five Ways (WR) and Owen St. (LMR). The Great Bridge stations were now South (WR) and North (LMR). Bilston was blessed with two stations, both with the same name although both had been in Great Western ownership since 1863. The main line

station became Bilston Central; the station on the Oxford Worcester & Wolverhampton line became Bilston West. Dudley station was, in effect, two stations working side by side. It continued to have two ticket offices, two goods sheds and now two names, Dudley Castle (WR side) and Town. This flurry of activity left Birmingham Snow Hill untouched, where the principal nameboards continued to show 'Birmingham' only, just as those at Low Level displayed only 'Wolverhampton'.

From 1952 station signs were modernised. The large wooden nameboards beloved of the Great Western, with raised lettering, were replaced with vitreous enamel versions in chocolate and cream. This did not happen overnight. Even Snow Hill had to wait until 1956, whilst Old Hill was still clinging to the old boards in 1964. These advised people to change for Halesowen, which had lost its public passenger trains in 1927. Ex-GW platform benches remained and a few were even updated with BR(W) cast into the legs. Modern replicas of both sorts of bench, with inferior wood, can be found on the present Snow Hill station.

An early sign that we now had a national rail network was the use of a BR symbol - another totem - on posters, time-tables, etc. Sometimes known as the 'hot dog' or 'sausage roll' it rapidly became familiar on station name signs throughout the country, as typified by the example seen at Four Oaks. These totems, which are now collectors' items, were in regional colours, small enough to be mounted on walls or lamp standards, yet clear enough to be seen easily from an arriving train. At first the regional boundary on the Birmingham-Bristol main line was at Church Road Junction, where the branch for Central Goods left the main line south of the then-closed station at Five Ways. All the local stations from Selly Oak to Barnt Green were fitted with WR totems, which were scrapped and replaced when the regional boundary moved near the top of the Lickey Incline, between Barnt Green and Blackwell, in 1958. The Western Region, of course, had to be different. Each totem at Birmingham Snow Hill formed part of a larger cream disc which had a chocolate ring near its edge. Rebranding with the corporate image was not always treated with urgency, but neither was old stock wastefully discarded. Some local stations, for example, continued to issue ex-GW and ex-LMS season tickets until at least 1957.

Webb 5' 6" tank engine No.46712 pauses at Great Bridge North with the 1.42pm Walsall-Dudley train, 12th May 1950.

(John Edgington)

5185 with a Dudley-Snow Hill train at Great Bridge South on 20th August 1957. Two of the three signal arms have the less conventional 'kidney' lamp spectacles, almost detached from the arms itself.

(John Edgington)

All these changes could only be cosmetic. They did not improve the actual service to the passenger or freight user. So how were the local train services improved at this time? They were not. Local trains were infrequent and slow, always steam hauled and often grubby, attracting less than 4% of commuters. Soho, a little-used station on the Stour Valley Line, closed in 1949; no new stations were opened. Bus services, almost without exception, ran at regular intervals. This applied to the intensive city routes but also to some rural workings (eg; Pelsall-Aldridge) even if that only meant "once every two hours". There were no regular interval local trains whatsoever, save for an hourly link between Walsall and Sutton Park, which ran on summer Sundays only!

Railway posters were frequently good quality, continuing a tradition of modern popular art which had flourished during the 1930s and 40s. Attractive colour posters brightened up many drab local stations, advertising the delights of such places as Leamington, Stratford and Malvern. Actually working out how to get to these 'beauty spots' (as they were known) was quite a different matter. At many stations the time-table on display was an enlarged copy of the book version, often a complicated mixture of several routes, with little or nothing to show the difference between through carriages and connecting services. This was the way it had always been done and the need for change had not yet dawned on those who were doing it. It was no doubt fascinating to the sort of person who enjoyed fantasizing over ancient copies of "Bradshaw's Railway Guide" for hours on end, but to the ordinary passenger who just wanted to know the time of the next train, it was rather frustrating. Regular interval services began between New Street and Sutton Coldfield in 1955, gradually spreading to other lines. This, the 'remembered time-table' became easier to recall, one simple step toward making the trains easier to use. Gradually the written time-table was improved too. Sometimes different strands of the 'same' services were separated into different services and, crucially, there was an easy distinction in print between through trains and connecting services. By the early 1960s the layout of most railway time-tables could be understood more easily, both in books and handbills and at stations. It was to be the early 1970s however, before complete clarity of presentation was achieved at the larger stations, notably Birmingham New Street. Time-table boards often attracted a small knot of curious passengers, peering anxiously. They showed the departure of each train, with all its calling points; the easier modern practice is to group together all the departures for any given place.

Buying a ticket was the same as it had been in Victorian days. With the exception of a few halts, mainly on the North Warwickshire Line, every station was staffed even when very few trains stopped there. For those not travelling, access to the station, for one hour only, was by platform ticket, even at such a minor establishment as Bordesley. It cost one old penny (1d = 0.4p). At most stations the ticket window was a small opening, a hatch in the wall, sometimes low down so that most people had to stoop to shout through to the ticket clerk. When no trains were expected he could go into hiding by slamming down a wooden shutter, only to raise it grumpily for any unexpected caller. There were racks of different coloured Edmondson tickets for a wide variety of destinations, together with a supply of blanks for the more obscure parts of the system, to be hand written as required. (These once familiar tickets, along with their date-stamp machine operated by the clerk's knuckles, were the invention of Thomas Edmondson, stationmaster at Brampton Junction on the Newcastle & Carlisle Railway in the 1840s.) The size of the ticket window meant that clerk and passenger were largely invisible to each other. If either was hard of hearing or the clerk had to consult the hand written ledger for the fare to an

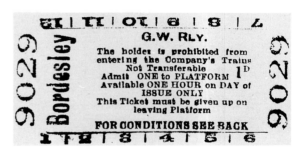

Great Western season ticket nine years late, and an Edmondson platform ticket for Bordesley. *(Robert Darlaston)*

unfamiliar place, an impatient queue could form rapidly. When hatches began to be replaced by larger windows - as at Coventry in 1962 - the passengers' first point of contact with the railway was radically improved. In that same year the booking office at Birmingham Snow Hill was the first to be equipped with a new German machine, capable of printing tickets as required from Edmondson blanks, so dispensing with the need for a large stock of pre-printed tickets. However, the clerk and his new machine remained firmly entrenched behind his white-tiled ticket window, scarcely larger or more attractive than the hole in the wall at any wayside station. Incidentally, 1962 saw another milestone for Snow Hill, as it became the first station in the Midlands to use the twenty-four hour clock on its time-tables.

One abiding memory from stations of the early 1950s is the smell. The Midland side of Birmingham New Street had a four road fish bay beyond the passenger platforms. This was in the Station St./Hill St. corner of the site, covered by a glazed ridge and furrow roof. The early morning smell emanating from the fish vans pervaded much of this side of the station. A train of up to six fish vans and perhaps two parcel vans, arrived in the bay very early in the morning, about 4am. The boxes of fish were offloaded and taken to the nearby wholesale market. The Saltley crew who worked the train, were always given a couple of good fish for their trouble. Later the same morning some boxes of fish found their way back to the station, where they would be transferred to the guards' vans of various passenger trains, including an early working to Redditch and Ashchurch via Alcester.

Birmingham suburban at the dawn of British Railways. A train for Lichfield simmers gently, while the crew of the New Street train waiting in the bay platform pose for the camera, obscuring the loco number in the process - Four Oaks, June 1949. The bench was a standard London & North Western Railway type. *(Author's collection)*

By the 1950s this loco, like many hundreds then in service, was of pensionable age, having been built to an 1885 design by Samuel Johnson of the Midland Railway. It carries the express passenger headcode and heads a train waiting at the 'fish bay' of the Midland side of the old New Street. Station Street is to the rear, with Sir Barry Jackson's Repertory Theatre visible behind the safety valve exhaust. *(Ken Wort)*

Far less pleasant was the frequent stink from the gentlemen's lavatories, mostly open to the sky for added ventilation. Those on New Street's Midland platforms dated from 1885. Unlike the Victorian urinal re-positioned outside the entrance to Jewellery Quarter station in 1995, they never achieved listed status!

Large areas of timber within a station readily absorbed the soot and steam, providing a distinctive background smell. This was especially true of the booking halls at Walsall and Sutton Coldfield, each with its system of wooden walkways leading to the platforms.

The smell of gas was accompanied by a faint hissing and burbling from the lamps at night. In the days before odourless North Sea gas, this coal gas was a mixture of hydrogen, methane and carbon monoxide. A small pilot light burnt permanently in every lamp. At dusk a porter walked along the platforms, lighting each lamp by pulling one side of a 'switch' and extending the gas supply to the two mantles. This switch was a metal arm on a central pivot, with a wire hanging from each end terminating in a loop. The process was reversed after the departure of the last train of the day. Lamps within reach could be lit unofficially at any time of day by the stray hands of passing boys. Most small stations, some medium ones and even the biggest - the Midland side of New Street - continued to be lit by gas until the 1960s, well after the rest of the country had progressed to electricity. The most extreme example of under-investment in lighting was on the Birmingham-Coventry line at Berkswell (Berkswell & Balsall Common as it then was), which continued to be lit by oil lamps until electrification of the line in 1967.

While just 4% of people in the West Midlands used rail on a regular basis it was rare indeed to encounter anyone who had never been on a train journey. The network still served the whole country and, as the first edition of the "Guinness Book of Records" (1954) stated, *The place farthest from a railway station in England is Lynton in North Devon. It is 18 miles from Barnstaple station".* (Lynton was briefly the terminus of a scenic narrow-gauge line from Barnstaple, which closed in 1935.) The fact that Lynton remained small and undeveloped was no coincidence. Most coastal resorts still had a railway station and most people used the train to get there. Car ownership was low, wartime petrol rationing did not end until 1950, foreign holidays were few and mostly unaffordable. Long distance coaches were slow and the motorway network lay in the future. For all practical purposes, the seaside was the only place to go and the train was the only way to get there. Rail had a captive market which travelled in less than ideal conditions. The photograph of the crowds waiting for the "Cornishman" at Snow Hill tells its own story.

A large number of carriages of pensionable age was kept exclusively for holiday traffic. Some of these veterans were used only on the ten peak weekends of the summer. School holidays were virtually the same throughout the country and most factories in the West Midlands shut down for the same fortnight every year. Everyone spent the first Saturday of the holiday 'getting away from it all' accompanied by everyone else. Overcrowding was routine, some people passing the whole journey between the Midlands and South Devon sitting on suitcases in the corridors. Every available locomotive, no matter how remotely suitable, was pressed into service. Late running was commonplace. This combination of vintage stock and unusual motive power was a feast for the eyes and cameras of enthusiasts, but not much fun for those on board. Such travelling conditions were a legacy of wartime, when they were tolerated, but they were now increasingly unacceptable. For many families, the holiday journey was an endurance test. The head of the household, circa 1952, may have been earning good money working in industry, especially the booming car industry, perhaps on the assembly line at "The Austin", Longbridge. He could possibly afford to buy, rather than rent, his own home. The family luxury may have been a new television. His only experience of rail travel consisted of two journeys per year, which were in old grubby carriages. The trains were late, refreshments non-existent, the loos were out of toilet paper or occupied by people travelling without tickets, there was nothing for the kids to do and a seven hour journey seemed like seven days. No wonder that he gritted his teeth, cursed British Railways, and promised himself that, having built cars for fifty weeks of the year, next time he'd save up, buy one and take the family away in that instead! The later joys of the Exeter Bypass, the M5 and strikes by Spanish air traffic controllers were unforeseen in 1952.

Real Improvements

Early improvements apparent to passengers after 1945 were mostly attempts to heal the scars of war, with one startling exception. Despite the harsh times, F.W.Hawksworth, Chief Mechanical Engineer of the Great Western, was able to build two new restaurant cars for the Birmingham main line. They seated 12 first class and 32 third class passengers and entered service on 31st December 1945. The Birmingham based car left Snow Hill on the 11.45am, returning from Paddington at 6.10pm. Passengers probably felt more comfortable with these vehicles than with the food available in them, as post-war shortages resulted in the frequent appearance of whalemeat on the menu.

Snow Hill's glass roof had been badly damaged during the air raids of April 1941. Emergency repairs were carried out immediately, but complete reglazing was not undertaken until 1946. Over at New Street, Cowper's great roof over the LNWR platforms had been removed by the end of 1947, thanks to general deterioration and the effects of several bombing raids between 1940 and 1942. It was replaced during 1948 with steel girder and asbestos roofing over the individual platforms. A small book, "The Story of New Street", by F.W.Grocott, was issued by the LMR in 1954 to commemorate the station's centenary. The new work was described as *"awning roofs of a temporary nature"*. Cheap, simple, crude even, they let in more light than the old roof - grubby since the 1920s, covered with tar-coated hessian during the war - and they certainly let in more light than the present day concrete blanket.

Due to the huge backlog in locomotive and track maintenance, it was five years after the end of the war before there were any real improvements to the rail link with London. October 25th 1950 saw the inaugural run of a completely new named train, "The Midlander". This restaurant car express linked Wolverhampton High Level, Birmingham New Street and Coventry with Euston. The first train steamed into New Street at 11.00am behind rebuilt Royal Scot 46140 "The King's Royal Rifle Corps", with a rake of eleven coaches freshly painted in blood and custard, to be greeted by the Lord Mayor. The state of the track was such that the train was timed to take 2 hours 40 minutes between Euston and New Street, 45 minutes longer than expresses in 1939. In the ensuing years "The Midlander" was speeded up as conditions improved. By 1958 the down train (ex-Euston at 5.40pm) was due in New Street at 7.47pm, continuing to Wolverhampton (arr.8.27) via the Grand Junction and a stop at Bescot (8.14). The up service used the Stour Valley route, arriving in Euston at 1.40pm, 2 hours 10 minutes after leaving New Street. This was the fastest steam-hauled link between Euston and New Street from the end of the war to the start of electric services in 1967.

Holiday crowds await the arrival of "The Cornishman" at Birmingham Snow Hill, 24th July 1954.

(courtesy of Birmingham Post & Mail)

6th September 1952 seemed to be a busy day for vintage rolling stock. Seen on a West Of England train at New Street's Platform 10 was this ex-Midland & Great Northern corridor carriage in a yellow-green livery. The second vehicle is an ex-North Eastern Railway coach in teak. As well as these, the photographer also recorded a 1907 American Special Boat Train van in the fish bay, and ex-Highland and GWR stock on another West of England train. At Walsall on the same day he witnessed a train from the Sutton Park line containing an ex-LNWR corridor carriage, an LMS corridor carriage of 1935 and a twelve-wheeled coach built for the Glasgow portion of the '2pm corridor' West Coast Main Line train in 1908. The loco in this shot, 4-4-0 No.41025 was shedded at Gloucester. *(F.W.Shuttleworth)*

The brand name starts here! The down "Inter-City" has just arrived at Wolverhampton Low Level from Paddington, about 1959, much to the delight of the boys gathered at the north end of the station. The locomotive with bell is, of course, 6000 "King George V".

(Martin W. Davies)

True to the spirit of the old companies, the Western Region was able to do better than this, restoring the 2 hour schedule first established between the two cities by the London & North Western Railway in 1905. Without realising it, the new train also lauched a now familiar brand name. The "Inter-City" began running on 5th October 1953, between Wolverhampton (LL) and Paddington. It was rostered for a "King" and the up train left Snow Hill at 9.00am, just as the down train left Paddington.

Hill Street and Navigation Street crossed the New Street station area on substantial bridges, constructed along with the original station. Although strengthened periodically as road traffic increased, they were life expired. Such was the state of the Hill Street bridge that it was closed in 1943. A temporary bridge was built alongside, but it remained unused until the end of the war because of a sharp turn at one end, too dangerous to use during the blackout. Work on a permanent bridge lasted from February 1948 until October 1951. Work then started on a new Navigation Street bridge, which was completed in December 1953. The size and substance of these bridges were not obvious from the roadway; casual visitors may not have realised that they were on a bridge. The Hill St. bridge was 42' wide and 150' long. The Navigation St. bridge was 60' wide, resting on two main girders, each 133' long, 12' deep and weighing 133 tons.

Within New Street station, colour light signals replaced the semaphores controlled from the famous No.3 box, on the footbridge, when that box closed in 1946. More colour lights were added on the Midland side in 1952, by which time all the station's platform lines were track circuited. It may seem surprising now, incredible even, but between 1951 and 1954 more improvements were carried out at New Street than at any other station in the West Midlands, barely ten years before the whole structure was swept away. The station was completely repainted in regional colours, a task which took two years. New signs and totems were installed throughout. The right-of-way footbridge was given new decking, a roof (on the LNW side) and side

panelling, on which numerous advertisements added welcome splashes of colour. Neon lighting was added to the station name on the Stephenson St. entrance, above a large new electric clock. Two new ticket offices on the footbridge eased the pressure on the main one at the gloomy Stephenson St. entrance. Both refreshment rooms were remodelled as cafeterias, what today would be termed 'fast food outlets'. Commuters on Platforms 1-3 (one through platform and four bays, 1, 1A, 2, 2A) had the benefit of prototype next train platform indicators, installed in June 1955. Well before the era of platform monitor screens, they each consisted of a white roller blind mounted in a large cabinet backlit by internal fluorescent tubing. The times and destinations of trains from these platforms were printed on each blind, which was rolled round by a porter to expose new trains as required. The old fingerposts and dummy clocks continued in use elsewhere on the station and train announcements not scrambled by the acoustics were often drowned by the sound of locomotive exhausts.

By 1954 New Street was issuing 3 million tickets a year. There were 8 through platforms (3-10) and five bays (those above plus No.11) which handled *"some 190 trains a day coming into the station and over 180 going out, and eight trains can use the station at one time"*. These figures apparently ignored empty carriage stock workings, making it appear as if 10 trains per day disappeared into some kind of black hole. The present station handles over 700 train movements per day, and some observers may well comment that they all disappear into a black hole! Movements within the 1954 station were controlled from six signal boxes (Nos.1, 2, 4, 5 & 9), with 382 levers between them. No.5, the biggest box, controlled all movement at the Wolverhampton end of the station, had 153 levers and required three men to work it. The smallest box was No.9, controlling bay platforms 1 and 1A, with 18 levers. The station provided employment for 600 people.

The view from the Queen's Hotel, 13th April 1960. A Park Royal dmu rests between duties in the LNWR side of the station. The Midland platforms are under the overall roof to the left, the rebuilt Navigation St. and Hill St. bridges can be seen to the right.

(courtesy of Railtrack)

Birmingham New Street's famous footbridge, refurbished after the war, showing the section spanning Queen's Drive, which still had its mid-section canopy at this time, 13th April 1960.

(courtesy of Railtrack)

"Jubilee" 4-6-0 No.45721 "Impregnable" waits at the Euston end of New Street with a London express, 1953. Eight years after the end of the Second World War and one of Britain's major stations remains patched up and forlorn. The sun may be shining but the whole scene seems to be covered in a layer of grime which, like the locomotive, is impregnable.

(Ken Wort)

A Birmingham scene rich in transport history, taken from the Queen's Hotel. In the foreground there are vans in the freight only 'coffee bay', in front of the signal box. Beyond Queen's Drive a 4-4-0 leaves the Midland side of the station. A steady procession of buses heads up Hill Street as trams for the Bristol Road routes wait by their shelters in Navigation Street, where an early split windscreen Morris 1000 hides behind a bus. This picture could not have been taken before work began on the Navigation St. bridge in October 1951 (right), nor after closure of the Bristol Road tram routes in July 1952.

(Maurice Newman collection)

F.W. Grocott concluded his centenary book thus - *"Another plan is being considered at present. This is the modernisation of the Stephenson Street entrance and ticket hall which, if it comes to fruition, will involve a further heavy expenditure."*
Two paragraphs earlier he had commented - *"Many plans have been considered in more recent times to improve the station structure but there have always been physical difficulties which it has been impossible to overcome, the principal one being its situation; for while there is the great advantage of its central position, that very fact precludes any major rebuilding."*
If only he had known what was to come .....

As signalling equipment reached the end of its useful life, it was renewed piecemeal, on a like for like basis. Some replacement manual boxes had very brief lives before the commissioning of the 1960s power boxes at New Street, Saltley, Coventry, Walsall and Wolverhampton. The new No.3 box at Bescot, at the north end of the station, dated only from 1953. At Smethwick, the ex-LNWR box, complete with skyscraper signals alongside, was a working ruin by the time it was replaced. Most unusual was the replacement box at Selly Oak, alongside the ex-Midland Railway structure. At the time this was part of the Western Region, so the new box was built to the standard WR pattern. It was commissioned on 19th January 1958, just before the regional boundary change. Snow Hill North, an early power box from 1909, was replaced by a new box in 1960, just seven years before the station closed to main line trains.

New BR coaching stock had all-steel bodies. The Standard main line corridor coach, later known as the Mark I, was based on the last LMS type. It came in two guises, a compartment coach with side corridor, and an open coach with centre aisle. However, restrictions on the use of steel were still in force and the budget for new passenger stock was limited. By the end of 1954 relatively few Mark Is had been built, only 1,800 at a time when the total carriage fleet numbered 37,000 - of assorted origin and uncertain vintage. When new, the Mark I interiors were lined with a wood veneer, often pale and bland, with a small plastic label naming the type of wood and its country of origin. Small numbers of non-corridor suburban coaches continued to be built until as late as 1960. They too had steel bodies, but in most other respects were simply updated versions of the classic railway carriage familiar to late Victorian travellers. They had heavy slam doors, upholstered bench seats, high luggage racks and at least one mirror. Heating was by piping under the seats, provided by steam from the locomotive. New stock, unlike the old, was not inclined to leak steam both inside and out. Ventilation was by the window in each door. In older stock the window frame rested on a ledge. A leather strap with holes at regular intervals was fixed to the base of the frame. A tug at the strap removed the window frame from the ledge; it could then be lowered into the door cavity, with the passenger placing one of the strap holes over the lug in the door frame. In the steel bodied stock, the window was lowered by downward pressure on the metal strip at its top. This type is still in service on more recent vehicles, including the High Speed Train.

If the first generation of BR carriages, main line and local, were modest developments of earlier types, they were none the worse for that. Everybody, as yet, had a clear view through a window, nobody had to face the back of another seat and cycles, prams, etc. could still be stowed in a guard's van.

New locomotives offered some surprises. At a time when the advantages of electric and diesel traction were becoming increasingly obvious abroad, BR opted to continue with steam. The reasons for this are complex and still a matter for some debate. Here, I merely outline some important points. Experience with main line diesels, in 1950, was limited to just *two*

locomotives, 10 000 and 10 001, familiar sights along the Trent Valley since 1948. Each was less powerful and more costly to run and maintain than a single "Coronation" Pacific. Experience of main line overhead electrification was non-existent until services began on the now-lamented Woodhead route between Manchester and Sheffield on 3rd January 1955.

Earlier, in 1943, Sir Alan Mount, a member of the maintenance division at the Ministry of Transport, summarised the likely post-war situation thus, *"for a country which produces excellent steam coal, but has to import oil, the advantages of imported fuel must be overwhelming before its general use can be justified."* In 1945, the mere suggestion that one or more of the railway companies might be tempted to order a few production main line diesel locos from General Motors provoked a stern reaction from H.M.Treasury, which opposed *"any proposal for the substantial changeover of main line railways in this country to oil-fired engines"*. This single sentence showed both the Treasury's ignorance of the workings of the railway and their ability to deny it financial resources. These characteristics have remained largely intact in subsequent years. In the context of the time however, the attitude of Sir Alan Mount and the Treasury was correct, given that this country had a thriving coal industry directly employing over half a million men and that North Sea oil was unknown.

In the immediate post war years some members of senior railway management did not see a large role for diesel. Main line steam, it was thought, would be replaced by main line electrification (if only!). In the meantime, it was reasoned, before the country could afford the high initial cost of electrification and while the necessary expertise was being gathered, why not fill the gap with more steam? Robin Riddles, the member of the Railway Executive responsible for mechanical and electrical engineering, was an unashamed steam enthusiast. Thanks to him, large numbers of new steam locomotives were built. Between 1948 and 1953 no fewer than 1,487 engines were constructed to pre-nationalisation designs, LMS "Flying Pigs", Great Western "Castles" and "Halls" among them. Riddles' team produced designs for 12 new classes of Standard steam loco, of which 999 were built between 1951 and 1960. For ease of access and maintenance they all had high running boards, well clear of the driving wheels. This family likeness gave them an instantly recognisable different appearance from other designs, with the exception of Ivatt's late LMS work. Some Standard classes soon became familiar on West Midland metals. The Class 5 mixed traffic 4-6-0s (numbered 73xxx) were virtually updated Stanier 'Black Fives', the design of which dated from 1934. Regular visitors to New Street, they could often be seen hard at work on the Bristol-Derby main line. A Birmingham Trades Council research team, known excitingly as Unit 53, published an article in "The Birmingham Journal" (according to the "Birmingham Post", 5th October 1953) indicating that train crews disliked the new 73000 Class 5, *"It is true that unions were consulted on footplate fittings but the engine is severely criticised for performance and footplate draughts due to the style of streamlining. Here is a practical question which demands closer liaison between drivers and firemen and loco engineers when the designs are still on the drawing board."*

The new Western Region signal box at Selly Oak, alongside the ex-Midland Railway box it replaced on 19th January 1958, seen six days earlier. Midland Railway 0-6-0 'chaffcutter' No.43435 stands alongside with a short local trip working, the only loco of that type with a high sided tender.   *(Roger Shenton)*

Black Five No.45033 on an express goods from Wolverhampton passing the No.3 signal boxes at Bescot, the new box under construction, mid-1953.   *(Ken Wort)*

Smaller classes, both tender and tank engines, were built for mixed freight and branch line work, arriving on the scene just before this type of traffic began a steep decline. Most of the 12 Standard classes were successful and some examples are still running on preserved lines, hardly surprising given their relative youth. When the Jewellery Line opened between Snow Hill and Smethwick Junction in September 1995, it was fitting that on the gala day before normal services began, the trains were hauled by a Standard tank, No.80079, borrowed from the Severn Valley Railway.

Readers with some knowledge of the various classes of steam locomotive will be interested in the accompanying shed census, produced by Gerry Crow. Compiled with the assistance of Ian Allan shed books, plus his own schoolboy observations at the time, he estimates that they are accurate, as far as is possible, for his chosen census date of 10th March 1953. What emerges from these statistics is the sheer weight of numbers of locos required to run the railway, the antique machines still in service (see especially Bournville and Saltley) and the small numbers of new post-1948 locos. As yet, only Tyseley had such locos in any number. It was home to four "Modified Halls", six new tank engines of Great Western design, the first ten of the 2-6-2 Standard Class 3 mixed traffic tank engines, Nos.82000-82009, and three new diesel shunters.

Later in the 1950s, the most familiar Standard type in the Midlands, the last, the most numerous and unquestionably the most successful, was the 2-10-0 9F, of which 251 were built between 1954 and 1960. (For some reason, their numbers were not allocated in chronological order, so the last to be built, "Evening Star", was numbered 92220.) They were designed as heavy freight engines and for that they were ideal, capable of hauling a 1,000 ton train at over 50mph on level track - this at a time when most freight trains were still unfitted, without continuous brakes and therefore compelled to amble along at 30mph or less. The ten small driving wheels, with a diameter of only 5 feet, were designed to grip the track tenaciously with heavy loads. They were certainly not meant for speed. What nobody anticipated, probably not even Riddles himself, was their ability to handle passenger trains. The size of the wheels proved no obstacle to fast running. There were, according to O.S.Nock, *"at least two fully authenticated records available of 9F engines attaining maximum speeds of 90mph"*. Generally recognised as one of the finest classes of steam loco ever to run in this country, they were destined to have absurdly short lives. Brilliant they may have been, but not perfect. David Jopling, then firing out of Bescot, recalled that they were *"hard on the fireman because the far corners of the firebox were a long way from the doors and you could easily get your hands and arms burnt."*

This Indian summer for steam, which continued into the 1960s, could not last. It was indeed the unchanging face of the railway. In 1955 the Modernisation Plan was published, followed in 1963 by the Beeching Report. In the West Midlands, as elsewhere, they would change the railway completely.

Standard Class 5 No.73031 calls at Bromsgrove with a Gloucester-New Street train, Bank Holiday Monday, 5th August 1963.

(Michael Mensing)

British Railways 'Standard' heavy freight loco, 9F 2-10-0 No.92052, passes through Hazelwell station, on the Camp Hill Line, with a northbound train of empties, 16th September 1961. This loco had high-sided tender, carrying 5625 gallons of water and 8 tons of coal, not the more usual 10 tons. Such variants were often based on the Eastern Region, and it may have been working its way back there. Hazelwell station lasted only from 1903 until 1941. The platforms have since been removed and the station buildings have seen service as a bathroom furniture showroom.

(Michael Mensing)

Standard 9F 2-10-0 No.92120 spreads a thick blanket of soot over Knowle & Dorridge station, as it passes with a northbound part-fitted freight, 14th August 1959.

(Michael Mensing)

Shed Census, 10th March 1953

Locomotives built since 1948 are shown in bold type. Those built before the Grouping (pre-1923) and already more than 30 years old, are given in italics. Locos were given a power rating (0-9) and their normal traffic type - P (passenger), F (freight), MT (mixed traffic).

BR Standard 5MT No.75023 has been prepared at Saltley shed, ready to work a semi-fast train from New Street to Bristol Temple Meads, about 1960.
(Maurice Newman)

ASTON (shed code 3D) [LMR]
0-6-0 diesel-electric shunter (1945) 12088/89/90/95
2-6-2T : Fowler : Class 3MT (1930) 40051
2-6-4T : Stanier : Class 4MT (1933) 42441 42470 42489 42552
42616 42658
2-6-0 : Hughes/Fowler : Class 5MT 'Crab' (1926) 42782 42810 42921
2-6-0 : Stanier : Class 5MT (1933) 42946/47/48/51/54/57/58/63/66/74
0-6-0 : Johnson : Class 3F (1885) 43308
0-6-0 : Fowler : Class 4F (1924) 44120 44219 44302 44350 44354
44360 44517/25
4-6-0 : Stanier : Class 5MT 'Black Five' (1934) 44844 44872/76/97
45052/58/65/94 45114
45322/49/70/97 45418 45448
2-6-0 : Ivatt :Class 2MT (1948/51) 46427 46492
0-6-0T : Fowler : 3F 'Jinty' (1924) 47363
0-8-0 : Bowen-Cooke : G1 Class 6F (1912) 49089
0-8-0 : G2A Class 7F (rebuilt 1936) 49278
0-6-0 : Johnson : Class 2F (1917) 58180/82 58295
Total - 52 steam (5 : 45 : 2) + 4 diesel shunters.

BESCOT (3A) [LMR]
0-6-0 diesel-electric shunter (1952) 12091/92
2-6-0 : Hughes/Fowler : Class 5MT 'Crab' (1926) 42779 42853 42939
4-6-0 : Stanier : Class 5MT (1934) 44914 45310 45402 45439
2-6-0 : Ivatt : Class 2MT (1948) 46425/26/90
0-6-0T : Fowler : Class 3F 'Jinty' (1924) 47294 47382 47396
2-8-0 : Stanier : Class 8F (1935) 48120/75 48250/97
48310/18/35/66/75
48453/77 48514/56 48602/05 48713/22/25/27/33/52/55/62/66/67/69
0-8-0 : G2A Class 9F (rebuilt 1936) 48930/50/64
49009/21/45/63/77/99 49189
49202/16 49223/45/46/66 49308/13/27/28/54/61/67
0-6-0 : Class 2F (rebuilt 1917) 58273/77
Total - 64 steam (2 : 59 : 3) + 2 diesel shunters

Bescot, 28th May 1950. Super D No. 49246 and 2-8-0 No. 48518 are on the shed's disposal road, Super D No. 49240 has the wagons to the rear. *(F.W.Shuttleworth)*

An ex-LMS 2-8-0 displays its old number, with an 'M' underneath, Bescot, 15th August 1948. The tender belonged to ex-WD loco No.77145. *(F.W.Shuttleworth)*

BOURNVILLE (21B) [WR]

2-6-2T : Stanier : Class 3MT (1935)   40099
4-4-0 : Class 2P (1912)   40439/63
4-4-0 : Fowler : 3 cylinder Compound Class 4P (1924)   40917/28
41064/73   41117/56/94
2-6-4T : Fairburn : Class 4MT (1949)   42050   42186
2-6-4T : Fairburn : Class 4MT (1945)   42685
2-6-4T : Fowler : Class 4MT (1927)   42338
2-6-0 : Hughes/Fowler/BR : Class 5MT 'Crab'   42824/25
(these locos were rebuilt with experimental Lentz poppet valves in 1931,
and again with Reidinger rotary poppet valves in 1953)
0-6-0 : Johnson : Class 3F (1885)   43203/46/63   43355/59
43520/21/68/83   43668/75/87
0-6-0 : Fowler : Class 4F (1924)   44520
4-6-0 : Stanier : Class 5MT 'Black Five' (1934)   44811/21/69
2-8-0 : Stanier : Class 8F (1935)   48420   48523   48669
0-6-0 : Johnson : Class 2F (1875)   58126/38/43
Total - 38 (*15* : 21 : **2**)

BROMSGROVE (21C) [WR]

(The purpose of this shed was to provide bankers for the Lickey Incline)
0-6-0 : Johnson/Deeley : Class 3F (1885)   43186   43667
0-6-0T : Fowler : Class 3F 'Jinty' (1924)   47276   47301/03/05/08
47425   47502   47565
0-4-0ST : Drummond/McIntosh : Class 0F 'Caledonian Pug' (1885)
56020
0-10-0 : Fowler : 'Big Bertha' (1919)   58100
Total - 12 (*4* : 8 : **0**)

COVENTRY (2D) [LMR]

2-6-0 : Ivatt : Class 2MT (1950)   46445/46
0-8-0 : G2A Class 7F (rebuilt 1936)   49330
0-8-0 : Bowen-Cooke : G2A Class 7F (1921)   49417   49441/42/44/46
0-6-0 : Class 2F (rebuilt 1917)   58217   58278   58293   58306
Total - 12 (*9* : 1 : **2**)

KIDDERMINSTER (85D) [WR]

0-6-0PT : Class CMPD 2F (1902)   No.29
(ex-Cleobury Mortimer & Ditton Priors Light Railway, converted from a
Manning Wardle saddle tank)
0-6-0PT : Dean : Class 2021 2F (1897)   2101
0-6-0PT : Collett : Class 5700 4F   7700   8718/27 (1927) : 3601 (1933)
2-6-2T : Collett : Class 5100 4MT (1929)   4100/53   5110   **4175 (1949)**
2-6-2T : Collett : Class 4500 4MT (1927)   4578/96   5518
2-6-0 : Churchward : Class 4300 4MT (1911)   6832
2-6-2T : Collett : Class 8100 4MT (1938)   8101
Total 15 (*3* : 11 : **1**)

MONUMENT LANE (3E) [LMR]

(with the passage of time Monument Lane itself became Monument
Road, the section crossing the railway has now been replaced by
Ladywood Middleway)
2-6-2T : Fowler : Class 3MT (1930)   40018
4-4-0 : Fowler : 3 cylinder Compound Class 4P (1924)   40933/36
41090
2-6-4T : Fairburn : Class 4MT (1945)   42262/63/64/65/67/74
2-6-4T : Stanier : Class 4MT (1935)   42579
0-6-0 : Johnson : Class 3F (1885)   43231
0-6-0 : Fowler : Class 4F (1924)   44057   44361   44506/12/14   44592
4-6-0 : Stanier : Class 5MT 'Black Five' (1934)   44942   45051   45390
0-6-2T : Webb : Class 2MT (1898)   46900
0-6-0 : Johnson : Class 2F (1885, some rebuilt 1917)   58117   58124
58178/79   58185/86
0-6-2T : Webb : Class 2F 'Webb Coal Tank' (1882)   58900
Total 30 (*9* : 21 : **0**)

Kidderminster's sorry looking engine shed (85D) had been in situ less than twenty years when this photograph was taken on 12th November 1950. It was to be found alongside the Bewdley branch, replacing an earlier shed at the station and opening in 1932. The steel and corrugated iron building seen here was first built to serve as the shed for Bassaleg, South Wales, in 1921. This two-road shed normally housed up to sixteen locos, most of which were employed on the Severn Valley and Tenbury branches.

(the late G.F.Douglas; R.K.Blenkowe

The ex-LNER 2-8-8-2 Garratt loco was shedded at Bromsgrove during 1949 and again in 1955 whilst it acted as a Lickey banker. It is seen being coaled up at Bromsgrove, 1949. The men in front of the wagon are shovelling coal onto a belt which conveys it to the coaling stage above the hungry monster's tender.   *(Roger Carpenter collection, courtesy Don Powell)*

Bromsgrove coaling stage, 28th April 1957. GWR 0-6-0T No.9432 arrived in June 1956 to assist the ailing Jinties in their banking duties, it was joined by two more ex-GWR tanks in January 1957. The famous Lickey Banker, Big Bertha, was withdrawn in May 1956 but Standard 9F No.92079, which had arrived in 1955, inherited Bertha's headlamp. Steam banking up the Lickey finished in March 1962.

(Roger Shenton)

The roundhouse at Saltley, still showing signs of war damage to the roof, viewed from the top of the coaling stage, early 1950s.

(T.G.Wassell, "Photos from the Fifties")

Before 1948 the GWR had a fleet of diesel railcars and the LMS had a number of diesel shunters. Two of the latter, 7126 and 7128, are seen at Saltley shed in early BR days, 6th June 1948. Their BR numbers were 12039 and 12041, as listed below. Both locos were withdrawn in October 1968.

(Roger Shenton)

SALTLEY (21A) [LMR]
0-6-0 diesel-electric shunter (1945)   12039-44 (6 locos)
0-6-0 diesel-electric shunter (1953)   12059/60/61/62/74/75/76/77
2-6-2T : Stanier : Class 3MT (1935)   40115 40168 40175
4-4-0 : Class 2P (1912)   40511
4-4-0 : Fowler 3 cylinder Compound Class 4P (1924)   41180
0-6-0T : Johnson Class 1F (1878)   41879
2-6-4T : Fairburn : Class 4MT (1950)   42053/54
2-6-4T : Fowler : Class 4MT (1927)   42326/27/37
2-6-0 : Hughes/Fowler : Class 5MT 'Crab' (1926)   42758/64/90
42827/57 42900/03
rebuilt with experimental poppet valves in 1931 and 1953 - 42818/22/29
2-6-0 : Ivatt : Class 4MT (1948)   43013 43046
0-6-0 : Johnson, ex-S & D : Class 3F (1896)   43201
0-6-0 : Johnson : Class 3F (1885, some rebuilt)   43210/14/23/84
43339/74/81 43433/35/41/43/84/90 43507/23/44/94
43620/24/27/44/73/74/80/84/90/93/98 43762

0-6-0 : Deeley : Class 3F (1906)   43791 43812
0-6-0 : Fowler : Class 4F (1924)   43843/45/55/58/62/65/69/75/78/79/91
43909/11/12/38/39/40/41/46/49/51/63/85/86
44004/23/26
0-6-0 : Fowler Class 4F (1924)
44049/84/88/92 44108/37/38/50/65/76/79/84/85/87/90
44201/03/04/11/13/24/26/27/35/48/63/89 44333/62
44406/13/18/27 44515/16/38/71/80/91
4-6-0 : Stanier : Class 5MT 'Black Five' (1934) 44659/60/66
44804/10/13/14/41/42/52/88 44919/20/62/66 45040/59
45186 45265/68/73/74 45447
0-6-0T : ex-S & D : Class 3F 'Jinty' (1929) 47313
0-6-0T : Fowler : Class 3F 'Jinty' (1924) 47638
2-8-0 : Stanier : Class 8F (1935) 48319/31/36/39/51/88/97 48417/24
48647/87 48700/63
0-6-0 : Johnson : Class 2F (1875) 58167 58230/61
Total - 169 (62 : 103 : **4**) + 8 diesel shunters (4+**4**)

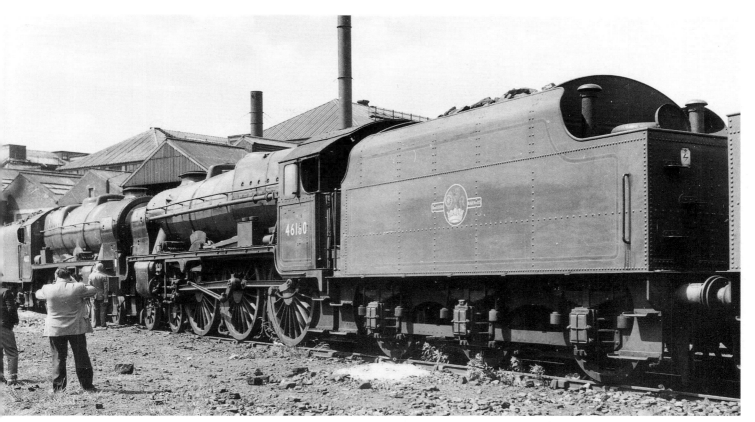

Saltley, 15th September 1963. In focus are two members of the ex-LMS "Royal Scot" class - 46152 "The King's Dragoon Guardsman" and 46160 "Queen Victoria's Rifleman". 46160's tender bears the second form (1955) of the British Railways lion - red, fierce and encircled, erupting from a crown and brandishing a railway wheel in its paws. Saltley closed to steam traction on 6th March 1967, the day through electric services began between Euston, Birmingham and the North West.   *(Joe Moss : Roger Carpenter collection)*

Bushbury shed, Wolverhampton, in the twilight of its years, 22nd April 1962.   *(Roger Carpenter collection)*

STOURBRIDGE (84F) [WR]

Ex-GWR streamlined diesel railcars - Nos.8 14 (1936) 29 (1940) 33 (1941)

4-6-0 : Hawksworth : County Class 6MT (1945) 1022

0-4-2T : Collett : Class 1400 1P (1932) 1414/38/58

0-6-0PT : Hawksworth/BR : Class 1600 2F (1949) 1619/21

0-6-0 : Collett : Class 2251 3MT (1930) 2209/32/46/70/79

2-8-0 : Collett : Class 2800 8F (1938) 2885 3821/27

2-8-0 : Robinson GCR : ROD 7F (1911) 3028

0-6-0PT : Collett : Class 5700 4F (1929, 1933 1936)
(1929) 5719/26/54/94/95 7705 8704/42 : (1933) 3649/58/67
3710/43/51 4646/87/96 8791/92/97 9613/36 9719/67/82
(1936) 7402/28/29/30/32/35/41/48/49

2-6-2T : Collett : Class 5100 4MT (1929) 4104/46/50
5101/05/07/55/65/67/70/80/89/91/97/99 **4173 (1949)**

*2-6-0 : Churchward : Class 4300 4MT (1911) 4375 5313/71/79
6327/32/54/91*

0-6-2T : Collett : Class 5600 5MT (1924) 5606/42/51/58 : (1927)
6609/46/67/74/77/78

4-6-0 : Collett : Grange Class 5MT (1936) 6803/28/57

0-6-0PT :Hawksworth/BR : Class 9400 4F (1949) 8419 9427/50/77

Total 96 (*15* : 74 : **7**) + 4 diesel railcars

TYSELEY (84E) [WR]

0-6-0 : diesel-electric shunter 13 000
(likely to be prototype for class below, according to 'Ian Allan' shed book of 1950. Formerly LMS machine No.7058, built 1934)
13 001 13002 13003 (built 1953)

0-6-0 : Collett : Class 2252 3MT (1930) 2203/38/57/96

2-8-0 : Churchward : Class 2800 8F (1903) 2826/48/49/56/67 Collett
(1938) 3829/37/39

2-6-2T : Collett : Class 3100 4MT (1938) 3101

2-6-2T : Churchward : Class 3150 4MT (1906) 3180

0-6-0PT : Collett : Class5700 4F (1933) 3625/50/53/57/60/73/89/93
3769 4648 8700 9608/10/14/35/80/82 9724/33/48/53/98

0-6-0PT : Collett : Class 5700 4F (1929) 5736/45/90 7713/35/58

2-6-2T : Collett : Class 5100 4MT (1929) 4110/11/16 5112
5152/56/63/64/66/98 **4170/72 (1949)**

4-6-0 : Collett : Hall Class 5MT (1928) 4964 5907/09/12/27 6904/38
: 6971 (Modified Hall, built 1944)

7912/13/18/29 (Modified Hall, built 1949)

4-6-0 : Collett : Grange Class 5MT (1934) 6843/53/58/66

*2-6-0 : Churchward : Class 4300 4MT (1911) 5333/69/70/86 6321/36
: 7317 (1925)*

0-6-2T : Collett : Class 5600 5MT (1927) 6630

0-6-0PT : Collett : Class 7400 2F (1936) 7438

2-6-2T : Collett : Class 3100 4MT (1938) 8108

0-6-0PT : Hawksworth/BR : Class 9400 4F (1949) 8415/63/68 9432

2-6-2T : Riddles : Class 3MT (1952) 82000- 82009 (10 locos)

Total 95 (*12* : 63 : **20**) + 4 diesel shunters (1+**3**)

WOLVERHAMPTON BUSHBURY (3B) [LMR]

0-6-0 diesel-electric shunter (1953) 12 093 12 094

2-6-2T : Stanier : Class 3MT (1935) 40122/25 40207

2-6-2T : Ivatt/BR : Class 2MT (1948) 41225

0-6-0 : Fowler : Class 4F (1924) 44027 44439/92

4-6-0 : Stanier : Class 5MT 'Black Five' (1934) 44829 45015 45287
45405

4-6-0 : Stanier : Class 6P 'Jubilee' (1934) 45688 45703/33/34/38/41
45742 - with double chimney, built 1936

0-6-0T : Fowler : Class 3F 'Jinty' (1924) 47397/98 47473

*0-8-0 : Bowen-Cooke : Class G2A 7F 'Super D' (1921, some rebuilt)
48940 49037/44 49106/25/67 49240/47 49416*

0-6-0 : Johnson : Class 2F (1875, rebuilt since) 58119 58152/83

Total 33 (*12* : 21 : **1**) + **2** diesel shunters

WOLVERHAMPTON OXLEY (84B) [WR]

*2-8-0 : Churchward : Class 2800 8F (1903) 2830/33/54/82
3802/13/25/60/63 (1938)*

2-8-0 : Robinson GCR : Class ROD 7F (1911) 3016/31/47

0-6-0PT : Collett: Class 5700 (1929, 1933) 3744/45/92/93 574448
7759/96/97 8798 9714/15/30/39/47/52/68/69

*2-6-0 : Churchward : Class 4300 4MT (1911) 5341/75/91
6335/61/63/96 9312/14 (1932)*

4-6-0 : Collett : Hall Class 5MT (1928) 4919/24/26/43/50/55/59
5944/45/66/72/91/20/42

Modified Hall 6975 (1944) **7915 (1949)**

4-6-0 : Collett : Grange Class 5MT (1936) 6854/56/62/79

4-6-0 : Collett : Manor Class 5MT (1938) 7818

0-6-2T : Collett : 5600 Class 5MT (1924) 5684 6610/40/45

0-6-0PT : Hawksworth/BR : Class 9400 4F 9408 (1947) **8417/28
(1949)**

2-8-0 : Riddles : Class WD Austerity 8F (1943) 90284

Total 67 (*14* : 50 : **3**)

WOLVERHAMPTON STAFFORD ROAD (84A) [WR]

4-6-0 : Hawkesworth : County Class 6MT (1945) 1004/17/18/19/29

2-6-2T : Collett : Class 3100 4MT (1938) 3102/04

2-6-2T : Churchward : Class 3150 4MT (1906) 3160

0-6-0PT : Collett : Class 5700 4F (1929, 1933) 3615/64 3756/78
9621 (1933) : 5701/38/39/80 8705/26/34 (1929)

4-6-0 : Collett : King Class 8P (1927) 6004/05/06/11/16/20

4-6-0 : Churchward : Star Class 5P (1907) 4049/53/61

2-6-2T : Collett : Class 5100 4MT (1929) 4103/05/08/15/47
5106/51/87/88/90

4-6-0 : Collett : Hall Class 5MT (1928) 4918/91 5995 Modified Hall
6964 (1944)

4-6-0 : Collett : Castle Class 7P (1923-46) 4000/79/83/92
5008/10/15/22/27/31/32/45/53/70/88 **7026 (1948)**

0-6-0PT : Hawksworth/BR : Class 9400 4F (1949) 8411/62 9428/35

0-6-0PT : Collett : Class 6400 2P (1932) 6418

Total 64 (*4* : 55 : **5**)

MISTAKES

With the best will in the world, a few mistakes creep into every book. Volume One of "A Century of Railways" (1900-1947) was no exception. Confirmed errors are as follows:-

- front cover – The caption described the leading coach livery as blood and custard'. It was, in fact, an earlier variation of the old LNWR livery, called 'plums and spilt milk'.
- page 4-5 (map) – 'Spen Lane' station should be shown as Spon Lane.
- page 6 – The driving wheels of Johnson's 'Spinners' had a diameter of 7'4".
- page 8 – 23/4 hours should read 2³/₄ hours.

- page 11 – the 160 ton weight of the "City to City" express included four carriages plus restaurant car.
- page 26 – the upper photograph shows a train at the *south* end of Snow Hill.
- page 27 – upper photograph, the 3100 Class had smaller driving wheels than the 3150 Class, 5'3", rather than 5'8".
- page 45 – Big Bertha's tender held 4 tons of coal, not 13 tons.
- page 59 – the lower photograph shows a parcels train, not empty stock.
- page 69 – the electric locomotive is in standard Rail Blue livery.

[Diary : Notes : Steam Gives Way to Diesel : Western Blue : Made in Birmingham]

The last word in West Midlands suburban rail travel before the coming of the diesels. In 1954 an hourly push-pull service was introduced between New Street and Sutton Coldfield, soon extended to Four Oaks to satisfy passenger demand. This was the first regular interval local service out of Birmingham since the First World War. Here Ivatt 2MT 2-6-2T No.41223 leaves Four Oaks with its two-coach train early in 1955.

(Peter Myatt)

DIARY

1955

January 23rd - Diverted York-Bristol express crashed at Sutton Coldfield station, seventeen lives lost.

April 29th - First day of shuttle service, New St.-Castle Bromwich, for this year's British Industries Fair. Service provided by a brand new Derby Lightweight dmu.

1956

March 5th - Birmingham-Sutton Coldfield-Lichfield becomes the first local service in the Midlands to be converted to regular interval diesel operation.

1957

June 17th - Wholesale dieselisation of most local services based on Birmingham Snow Hill.

August 1st-12th - World Scout Jamboree in Sutton Park generates over 130 special trains between July 29th and August 14th.

September 14th - Last trains call at Winson Green station.

September 30th - Butlers Lane Halt opened, between Four Oaks and Blake Street.

1958

March - five hundredth diesel multiple unit built at Derby works.

May 10th - Birmingham Snow Hill - Cardiff General service began operation by new Swindon-built Cross Country dmus.

June 1st - First Motorail train from Sutton Coldfield to Stirling.

November 15th - Monument Lane and Pleck stations closed.

November 17th - New regular interval dmu service begins, Wolverhampton-Walsall-Lichfield-Burton.

1959

April 4th - Last train calls at Brindley Heath (opened 1939), between Hednesford and Rugeley.

1960

January 1st - Halesowen-Northfield workmen's specials final day of operation.

January 15th - Spon Lane station closed with effect from this date.

February 1st - Albion station closed with effect from this date.

February 14th - Bournville engine shed closed.

April - Hourly diesel service begins between Birmingham New Street and Redditch

September 12th - Inaugural run of the "Birmingham Pullman"

1962

1st March - Rebuilding of Coventry station officially complete.

July 28th - Last day of passenger services on the 'Old Worse & Worse' line between Priestfield and Stourbridge Junction.

September 10th - Snow Hill-Paddington service completely dieselised.

September 24th - £200,000 rebuilding of Tamworth station completed. This was a very busy station for mail interchange between the Birmingham-Derby and Trent Valley lines. Each night seven Travelling Post Offices called and up to 2,000 bags of mail were transferred. Rebuilding incorporated rooms for storing mail and a mess room for TPO crews who changed trains here.

October 10th - Wednesfield Heath station closed to goods, 92 years after closing to passengers. This was the original 'Wolverhampton' station of the Grand Junction Railway, opening with the line in 1837.

Following the tragedy of the Sutton Coldfield crash (Sunday 23rd January 1955), which claimed 17 lives, railwaymen worked round the clock to reopen the line to normal traffic. Services resumed on Wednesday 26th and on that day Stanier 2-6-4T No.42421 heads a local for Birmingham shrouded in steam. *(courtesy of Birmingham Post & Mail)*

Notes

The publication of "The Modernisation and Re-equipment of British Railways" in January 1955 - the Modernisation Plan - was a signal for change. That same month, the unchanging way in which the railway was run could be seen in the Sutton Coldfield accident of Sunday 23rd.

A York-Bristol express with three hundred people on board, diverted because of engineering work, failed to take the curve through the station. Nine of the ten carriages were derailed, the first four were totally wrecked. The loco, Stanier Black Five No.45274, ended up on its side on the down platform. Seventeen people died, including the fireman and pilot driver. Police were on the scene in moments, as the police station was just fifty yards away. The other emergency services began arriving within minutes. After 40 minutes a veritable army of emergency personnel were at the scene; 17 fire service vehicles, 16 doctors, a blood transfusion unit, a mobile surgical unit, 33 ambulances and 70 police officers. There were many acts of individual heroism. One passenger, Pilot Officer Kepczyski, a Polish veteran of the Battle of Britain, organised his RAF colleagues into a rescue team and worked with desperate energy until he collapsed.

Ticket collector Arthur Attenborough and fireman Derek Smith, both travelling to work, separately realised that a northbound train was due, ran past the wreckage to the signal box and together set the signals to danger. Marjorie Fairey, who heard the crash from her house near the line, jumped onto the track and frantically waved at the northbound train, which stopped 470 yards short of the wreckage. There must have been many other acts of personal courage which went unrecorded but were no less real for that. The team spirit of the emergency services was matched by that of the railwaymen who worked long hours in distressing conditions to remove the wreckage and reopen the line. Services were restored on Wednesday 26th and the accompanying photograph shows a Birmingham bound train that morning, standing in what is left of Sutton Coldfield station.

In the face of such tragedies as Sutton, railwaymen, the emergency services and ordinary individuals caught up in events can be relied upon, to use a hackneyed but appropriate phrase, to 'do their bit'. Here, in a crisis, the unchanging human spirit was seen at its best.

Drivers were required to have an accurate knowledge of the route over which they were travelling. If they did not 'know the road' they had to take a pilot driver on board and remain in the cab themselves. The driver of this express, having picked up a pilot for the unfamiliar part of his route, then chose to ride 'on the cushions' in the first carriage. For this he was criticised at the enquiry. The train crashed because it was travelling at about 60mph on a 30mph curve; as the pilot driver died we shall never know why he failed to slow down.

As a pedestrian, I know the way round my local town centre; as a motorist I know the road to a variety of places. Yet no matter how familiar I am with any route, I need signs, road markings and traffic lights in order to travel safely. On the railway, drivers were expected to know the whereabouts of every signal, crossing, curve, speed restriction, etc. by heart. In most steam locomotives speed had to be judged without the aid of a speedometer. There were no headlights for night running. These were unchanging railway practices in urgent need of attention. As a result of recommendations made by the official inquiry into the Sutton crash, warning signs were to be placed at curves where the permitted speed was lower than the general line speed. The signs show the speed limit in cut-out metal figures. They were first used on the LNER in the 1930s, but after Sutton no fewer than 11,250 new signs were needed! Evenso, railwaymen still had to rely heavily on knowing the road by heart, because if they remembered to slow for the curve only when they saw the sign, it was too late. Another accident on a curve through a station (Morpeth, Northumberland, May 7th 1969), which cost six lives, resulted in the next logical step, an advanced warning board for many speed restrictions, illuminated at night and reinforced with an audible warning in the cab. The railway was beginning to change.

Steam hauled push-pull trains began an hourly regular interval service between New Street and Sutton Coldfield (soon extended to Four Oaks) in 1954. The service was dieselised and the frequency doubled in March 1956. The growing fleet of new diesel multiple units soon spread to other local routes. New main line diesel locomotives began appearing at New Street before the end of the decade. Western Region local services based on Snow Hill were also dieselised although, as on the London Midland, steam was used into the 1960s to help with some of the heavier rush hour trains.

The "Midlander" and "Inter-City" had improved the link with London on both routes in the early 1950s. However, by 1955 the majority of trains on both routes, still all-steam, showed little improvement over their pre-war counterparts. For that year's summer time-table, noted the "Railway Magazine", there were four services in each direction which took 94 minutes for the 94 miles between Coventry and Euston. The 4pm departure from Snow Hill took 23 minutes for the 23.3 miles to Leamington Spa. These were the only trains on either route required to run at 60mph, start to stop. The Wolverhampton-Snow Hill-Paddington line service was speeded up when fully dieselised in September 1962. Two years earlier, and on the same route, the Blue Pullman had brought some much needed style and glamour to rail travel. This train, an express multiple unit, pointed the way to the High Speed Train of the 1970s.

The railway proved that it could still handle large numbers of people successfully, especially during the summer of 1957. The World Scout Jamboree was held in Sutton Park from 1st to 12th August. It attracted over 80,000 Scouts, and some Guides, and generated about 130 special trains, plus an augmented local service on the Sutton Park line. The busiest single day was Tuesday 6th August, when 30,000 Cubs descended on the park, 10,000 in coaches and 20,000 in 23 special trains. The number of car owners was growing relentlessly but the Suez crisis of 1956-57 posed a threat to oil supplies and saw the introduction of petrol rationing for a while. This helped to ensure that in 1957 the railways carried more holidaymakers between the Midlands and the West Country than in any year before or since. There was also a busy programme of day excursions, which ran throughout the summer at bargain fares. Some did not stray far, visiting the Severn Valley line, which was still part of the national network. Others brought day trippers into the area, chiefly to Cadbury's at Bournville and to Dudley Zoo.

The first Motorail service in the country began running between Sutton Coldfield and Stirling in the summer of 1958, although it was known as a Car-Sleeper train before 1967. It ran twice a week, with accommodation for 20 cars in covered vans and 84 passengers in sleeping berths. The return fare for car and driver was £14/10/- (£14.50) plus £5 for each additional adult. The first train left Sutton on Sunday 1st June and was hauled by Black Five No.45038. It was crewed as far as Derby by driver Eric Baxter and fireman 'Bunny' Kemp, aged just 28 and 17 respectively. The service was successful and the following year two Standard Britannia Pacifics, 70046 and 70048 (both built at Crewe in 1954) were transferred from Holyhead to Aston shed to handle these heavy trains. Over the next few years the popularity of the service grew, as did the number of trains, choice of destination - and the fare. The return fare for car and driver had risen to £19/10/- (£19.50) by 1961 and £22 by 1965, plus £2 extra for large cars and a further £2 surcharge for height of season travel! By the summer of 1972 Motorail trains, each with a capacity of 44 cars, left Sutton six times every week - for Stirling on Sundays, Mondays, Wednesdays and Thursdays, for Newton Abbot on Fridays and St.Austell on Saturdays. All departures were at 23.15, except for the Wednesday train (13.10). The Monday train also served Inverness. That season Sutton handled over 4,000 cars and 12,000 passengers. However, these Motorail trains finished for ever in September 1972. Crewe was to be developed to replace both Sutton and Newton-le-Willows. This deprived Midland motorists of a convenient railhead and a fast, user-friendly way of taking their cars on holiday, further evidence, if any were needed, of the lack of transport integration in this country. Motorail is now extinct in Britain, except for one short and very intensive service, Le Shuttle.

Some stations closed between 1955 and 1962. The Stour Valley line lost four little-used stations at Monument Lane, Winson Green, Spon Lane and Albion. The 1958-59 timetable shows that Stour Valley trains serving all stations left New Street at 06.30, 07.15, 08.35, 08.48, 12.15(SO), 13.10, 15.50, 16.59, 17.53 and 19.40 - hardly an inspiring incentive to use the railway.

The most important line to close to passengers was a section of the Oxford Worcester & Wolverhampton (OWW), between Stourbridge Junction and Priestfield. Bilston West, Daisy Bank & Bradley, Princes End & Coseley, Tipton Five Ways, Blower's Green and Round Oak closed completely. Some of these places had other stations on other lines, but Brierley Hill lost all its passenger trains with this closure. Its two stations, Brierley Hill and Brettell Lane, remained open for parcels and general goods. In its last years the line had seen few stopping trains outside the peak hours. In the summer 1958 timetable, for example, they left Wolverhampton at 06.32, 06.50, 07.35, 08.14, 16.52, 17.29 and 18.05. There were seven southbound locals on Saturdays and nine on Sundays.

(Text continues on page 36)

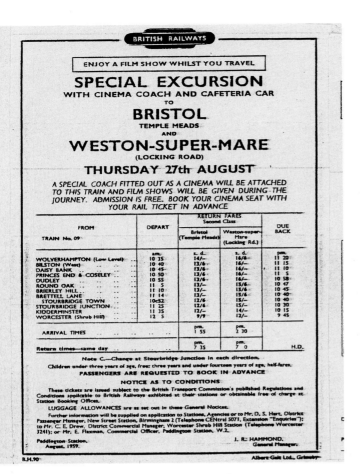

Ex-LNER No.61006, a 'Bongo', leaves Dudley at 5.15pm with a return excursion for Lincoln, 2nd April 1961. There were up to eight excursions at Bank Holiday times - see sidings - from places such as Lincoln, Nottingham, Leicester and Stoke. *(John Edgington)*

Jubilee No.45641 "Sandwich" enters Dudley with the 6.40pm return excursion to Nottingham, 2nd April 1961. *(John Edgington)*

(Opposite page) A selection of handbills for excursion trains, 1956-61. *(Robert Pearson collection)*

HOLIDAYS

On summer Saturdays surprising motive power could be seen on some long distance trains. A type more usually associated with freight, 4F 0-6-0 No.44424, climbs the Lickey Incline on 17th August 1957 with a heavy Bournemouth West to Nottingham Midland train, which was banked by two 0-6-0 panier tanks of Great Western design then shedded at Bromsgrove. 44424 was shedded at Gloucester and would have taken over the train there or at Bath Green Park (now a Sainsbury's store) after arrival off the Somerset & Dorset line. *(Robert Darlaston)*

Ex-LMS 2-6-4 tank No.42541, of a type designed by Henry Fowler in 1935, at Stechford on 31st October 1959. The train is a football excursion from Coventry to Witton, and is signalled for the direct line to Aston. Some of Stechford's extensive sorting sidings can be seen on the right, beyond the platform lamps, electric when parts of New Street were still gas lit. Whatever the hopes of the supporters on this train, they were to be unfulfilled. Coventry's away record against Aston Villa was very bad. For the whole of the twentieth century they failed to win a single game at Villa Park - until 14th February 1998, when they scored the only goal of the match.

(Robert Darlaston)

5088 "Llanthony Abbey" passes through Tyseley with a northbound holiday express.

(Jones family collection - courtesy of Locomotives International)

D5814 (later 31 414) approaches Lichfield City with an excursion for Dudley Zoo from Halifax and Rotherham (Masborough), 5th August 1962. This loco had a Mirlees 1470hp engine when new, a variation on the company's small fishing boat engine. The Mirlees 31s later had English Electric engines fitted, and some of the Mirlees originals did further duty in fishing boats. *(Roger Shenton)*

The OWW line, along with the neighbouring 'Bumble Hole' between Old Hill and Dudley, definitely missed out when other Western Region local services were upgraded and dieselised in 1957. The short stretch between Dudley and Blower's Green continued to be used by Bumble Hole trains until they ceased in 1964. Halesowen had been the first place of any importance in the West Midlands to lose its public passenger trains, in 1927, but workmen's trains from Halesowen, to serve 'The Austin' and its own station at Longbridge, just made it into the 60s. The last one ran on 1st January 1960, at a time before New Year's Day became a public holiday.

It was not all closure and contraction. Most local services were at least partially dieselised and began running to regular interval timetables. Some of these services patterns, such as Wellington-Wolverhampton LL-Snow Hill-Lapworth, have long since vanished.

In 1957 the almost unthinkable happened. A new station opened, Butlers Lane Halt. In 1938 the LMS produced plans for a station here. As there were virtually no houses in the area at that time it would have been a speculative venture, designed to entice potential commuters to a green field site. Plans for a station were put on hold by the war and in 1957, by which time the houses had already arrived, a more modest structure was deemed adequate. The "Birmingham Evening Mail" (30th September) reported -

"The first new railway station to be built in the Birmingham area since the war, Butlers Lane Halt, at Four Oaks, opened today. It serves a large residential area on both sides of the main Birmingham-Lichfield road. A temporary timber construction, with waiting rooms and ticket kiosk, it has taken almost six weeks to prepare."

Although temporary, it lasted until 1991, when it was replaced by a new station on the same site in conjunction with electrification of the Cross City Line. Seventeen years had passed between the building of Canley Halt in 1940 and the opening of Butler's Lane Halt. It was to be seventeen more years before the next new station in the area, Birmingham International, welcomed its first passenger.

On the freight side bigger, it seemed, was definitely going to mean better. In 1960 work started on the complete remodelling of the marshalling yard at Bescot. According to "Railway Magazine" it would cost £1.5million and take two years to complete. In reality, work was not completed until the autumn of 1965. Modernisation would mean the speedier marshalling and sorting of traffic, enabling a greater throughput of wagons. Manual signalboxes and shunt frames were to be replaced by a new control tower which, *"will be equipped for push-button sorting, with automatic operation of points and retarding apparatus, and will include staff amenity buildings and new lighting. When completed this yard will be capable of receiving, sorting and despatching over 3,000 wagons a day."* What was not foreseen at the time of this investment in new facilities was how quickly some of it would become obsolete.

With the swift reduction in wagonload traffic during the 1960s, adopted as British Rail policy, the useful life of the expensive retarders at Bescot was all too brief. More important, many men's useful working lives, on the railway at least, were also over. The improved efficiency at Bescot meant that other yards could be closed - *"At present, the area between Birmingham, Wolverhampton and Walsall is served by a number of marshalling yards of varying size, including those at Bushbury, Stechford, Wichnor and Birmingham Exchange, all of which will cease to be used for marshalling when the new Bescot yard commences operation".* (Railway Magazine)

During the 1960s all the area's main stations underwent some form of upheaval. For most it was not a happy experience, with one notable exception. The new station which emerged from the rubble was superior to the old. Although work was complete in 1962 this station is included in the next chapter, to set it alongside the others. Development had begun during 1957. The "Railway Magazine" (January 1958) noted, *"At Coventry the provision of a new parcels depot marks the first stage in the complete reconstruction of the station."*

The 'Old Worse & Worse' just before closure of its northern section. The 10.15 Wolverhampton-Stourbridge Junction leaves Dudley behind a 2-6-2 tank engine on 28th July 1962. Pigeon baskets were once an everyday sight at many stations, as here.

(Robert Darlaston)

Winson Green, on the New Street-High Level (Stour Valley) Line, one day in 1955. A new Park Royal dmu set is bound for Wolverhampton, while ex-LMS Fowler built (1927) 2-6-4T No.42309 enters the station with a local for New Street. The name board is set at an angle, the station is lit by gas, the electric lamps visible on Winson Green Road are typical of the 1950s, the bridge to the left spans Thomas Telford's 'Main Line' canal, while the slums await the bulldozers. *(Roger Carpenter collection)*

Fowler 2-6-2 tank (3P) of 1930 still carries its LMS number, 49, with an 'M' above it on the bunker side to show that it belongs to the London Midland Region of British Railways, 21st May 1948. The train was a Wolverhampton-New Street local, just leaving Monument Lane. The purpose of the high signal box was to enable the signalman to have a view of trains approaching from beyond the road bridge. *(H.C.Casserley; Roger Carpenter collection, courtesy Don Powell)*

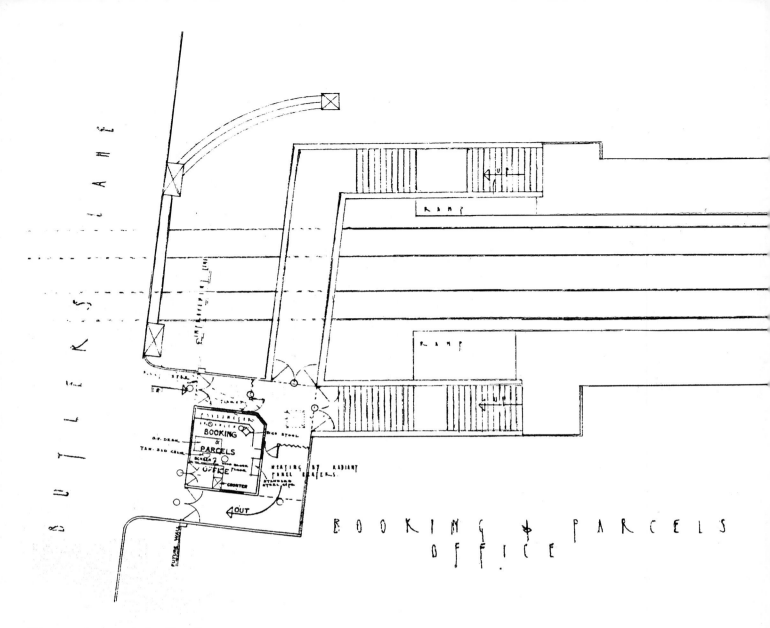

Steam gives way to diesel

Steam was still dominant in 1955. The introduction of new diesel types in succeeding years provided a steep learning curve for drivers and firemen. One of today's Bescot-based drivers with English Welsh & Scottish Railways (EWS) is Ray Churchill. He was a Bescot fireman during the transition period, steam finally leaving the shed in 1966. When the diesels were introduced he felt sorry for the older drivers - *"They had worked all their lives on steam, a fairly simple machine, then they were suddenly faced with the 'infernal combustion engine' and had to learn a lot of technical stuff which they didn't really want and didn't understand."*

One night he was second man in the cab of a new English Electric Type 4 (Class 40), hauling a freight train along the Sutton Park line towards Park Lane Junction and the sidings at Water Orton. There are several miles of downhill running from Sutton Park, except for a short stretch at Penns. With a slow steam loco, such as a Super D, it was often possible to coast down the grade without brakes. The technique for driving - and braking - a diesel was totally different. On this occasion the train was bowling along down the grade. Many of the wagons were fitted with vacuum brakes directly controlled from the cab. The driver, who was approaching retirement age, never touched his vacuum brake, but just used the straight air brake, which is for the locomotive only and does not brake the train at all. Worried, Ray walked through the 'boiler room' to the rear cab. Aware of some flashing outside, *"I put my head out and there were catherine wheels of sparks coming off the locos wheels and brake blocks as the weight of the train was pushing it from behind. The vacuum brakes were needed too"*.

Having arrived at Water Orton safely the loco detached from its train and went to the east end of the yard to run round and back up onto the rake of wagons that would form the return train. One characteristic of a Class 40 was that it never seemed to be satisified when starting from rest and the power handle was just in the 'On' position. *"The amps had to keep climbing"*, and it would tend to run away with itself, like a car with too much choke. This happened and the loco accelerated to 40mph (the yard limit was 10mph) and Ray, fearing a derailment, had to shout "Stop!" The driver applied the brake and did not seem to notice that anything had been wrong. Never having had a speedometer in a steam cab, he never looked at the one in the diesel. The riding quality in a new diesel was superior to any steam loco; 40mph, even within the yard, seemed smooth and slow; in the cab of a Super D or Class 8 it would have seemed like an earthquake. *"Such incidents were not uncommon with*

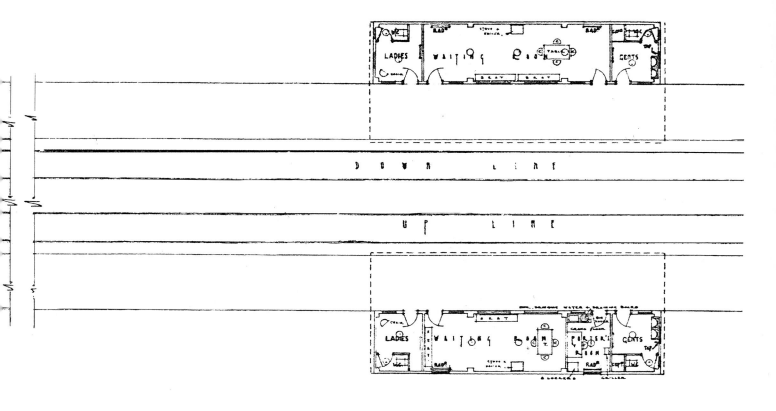

Butlers Lane opened in 1957, but these plans are of a station proposed for the same site in 1938. *(courtesy of Railtrack)*

some of the old boys and it was quite pitiful to see them handling the diesels at first".

One driver in particular was very wary of the Class 40s and their different braking characteristics. There is also a continuously falling grade when travelling over the Sutton Park line in the westbound direction, from Aldridge to Ryecroft Junction. When Ray once travelled over this stretch the driver in question held speed down to a 10mph crawl all the way. His excessive caution seemed vindicated a while later when a diesel-hauled unfitted freight lost control on this stretch and ran into the back of another train at Ryecroft.

Worries about braking with the new locos were very real, especially when many trains were still largely unfitted. As a steam fireman Ray used to go down the OWW through Dudley and Stourbridge to Hartlebury, with a train of slack for Stourport Power Station. This was downhill for most of the way, especially between Dudley and Stourbridge Junction, much of it at 1:75 south of Round Oak. With steam, and a rake of 16-ton unfitted mineral wagons behind, *"you used to go down there on your hands and knees"*. It was soon apparent that at least as much care was necessary with the new diesels, even where the grade was easier. Ray's driver, with a Sulzer 1160 (Class 24) was approaching Blakedown with a power station train when the distant signal was at caution. The brake was applied for a possible stop at the level crossing but the effort of braking, with the train pushing from behind, meant that the brake blocks caught fire although the train hardly slowed. Fortunately the Blakedown signal cleared, sparing the crossing gates from demolition.

There were one week learning trips for each type of loco, often involving a training run to Rugby with a three coach train. Ray was second man on a Class 40. On arrival at Rugby the loco would run round and set off back. "Easing up", before coupling up with a 40 was an interesting experience. *"You put the power handle to 'On' and held the speed down with a good dose of straight air brake. After stopping six feet off the coach buffers some of the learner drivers would keep opening and closing the power handle to keep the speed down. This practice was frowned upon as it mucked up the electrical contacts. The handling driver was doing this when the loco inspector said, "Come out of the seat, let me show you how it's done". He did. He didn't apply enough brake and we hit the coaching stock with a loud "Crump". No damage was done and no one said anything, but a lot of hand to mouth tittering went on".*

When diesels first came, reactions to them were almost as varied as the men who were to crew them. Some could not wait to see the back of steam whilst a few Bescot firemen, who were on the verge of passing out as drivers, left when they realised that steam would no longer be available. One extreme reaction occurred on the express fitted goods to London, the 'Camden'. One train crew - driver, fireman, guard - were delighted to find that a diesel had been rostered for the turn. As they lodged overnight however, Camden "borrowed" the diesel for an express passenger turn. When he discovered that a steam loco had been rostered for the return journey, and that he would actually have to do some work, the fireman refused point blank to work on steam again and returned 'on the cushions' from Euston. Camden had to supply one of their own men and the Bescot fireman was severely reprimanded.

The second man in the diesel cab, the ex-fireman, apparently just sat there. At the time there was much criticism in the press of extravagant overmanning, of the trade union tail wagging the management dog, etc. Second men were not strictly necessary and eventually they were phased out. However, to dismiss them in large numbers, simply because steam was in decline, would have wasted a large pool of talent and enthusiasm, as many second men had had a lot of training and would soon have been drivers in any event. Ray Churchill reckoned that most of Bescot's second men kept their jobs and went on to become drivers. In 1957 Ryecroft shed closed to steam and those drivers not required for the dmus were sent to Bescot. Jobs were allocated according to seniority and some Ryecroft men were older than the Bescot crews. This resulted in some Bescot drivers being put back to firing and some firemen being put back to cleaning. As sheds contracted or closed, men were displaced and some found permanent employment at Bescot, from Wolverhampton Stafford Road and Oxley, Rowsley, Derby, Aston, Monument Lane, etc. *Bescot became quite a cosmopolitan shed"*, said Ray. This of course stopped promotion at the bottom end of the scale and some young hands had to move away to keep their jobs. Ray Churchill was made redundant as a cleaner, receiving a letter telling him he would be transferred to Saltley the following week in order to remain in the line of promotion. Fortunately, Ronnie Ward, Bescot's branch secretary for ASLEF, got to hear of it. He went and told the shedmaster in no uncertain terms that while he was employing ex-drivers over the age of sixty-five to do shed labouring jobs, he could not make young cleaners redundant. Ray stayed at Bescot.

Horace Plant began his railway career before the war and finished it driving main line diesels. When he was a passed cleaner (ie; passed to act as a fireman before being fully qualified as such) there was an occasion in 1940 when he fired a long heavy freight, including munitions wagons, which left Rugby for Bescot at around 7pm. This was the night of 14th November, and at around 8pm it was put into the loop line south of Coventry at Brandon Ballast Pit. It was to remain there for over twelve hours. Horace and his driver spent much of that time crouched under the train, wearing tin hats, watching helplessly as the city was blitzed. It was, without doubt, the worst experience of his life.

Horace 'passed out' as a driver in 1948. With peace and nationalisation came the hope that conditions would improve and wages increase in line with those of other workers. They didn't. Having fired the Super Ds, *they were difficult to fire because of the long flat firebox and it was hard to get coal up front"*, he started driving on one of Bescot's new diesel shunters. These, of course, were one-man operated and bustled around incessantly, *"life was busy but boring, you never used to stop, there was supposed to be a twenty-minute break in the shift but you often couldn't have it"*. Outside the yard, and as steam declined, Horace often drove the new Type 2 Class 24 diesels on freight workings between Bescot and Crewe. These were soon christened 'Fruit Machines' on account of the control desk with its array of fault lights. Set at an angle of 45 degrees to the driver, it looked like a little one armed bandit.

David Jopling was a fireman at Bescot around 1963. He was in the relief link, meaning that he booked on as spare, ready for any turn that was offered. As a young man, still living at home, he was soon faced with plenty of work and ingrained prejudices. He was approached by the shed foreman who asked him if he was interested in a double trip, ie; a night away from home. He asked if he could let his parents know first and the foreman simply said, "I'll tell them". He was rostered for the overnight Camden freight and, on seeing him, his rather astonished driver did not speak. He clearly didn't fancy having to take such a young and

inexperienced looking fireman all the way to London and back. He rapidly disappeared to consult with the foreman, soon returning to say, "It looks as though I've got to put up with you." Aboard Black Five No.45410, they took the train out of the yard, the driver all the while telling Dave what to do and how to do it as though he were still a schoolboy. The journey passed, nervously for Dave, but without incident. On arrival at the lodge they had breakfast, prior to several hours sleep. During the afternoon the driver seemed to mellow, showing Dave some of the sights of London, before they had a meal and a pint together. On the return trip they settled into a comfortable routine from the start, the driver doing some of the coaling while Dave made the tea. But this was in the last years of steam, when locomotives were not always maintained in prime condition - to put it kindly. The injectors developed a fault at Hatch End, barely ten miles into the journey. The train stopped, the fire had to be put out and Dave spent much time on top of the boiler trying to close the clacks. Clack valves, it should be explained, are non-return valves usually fitted on top of the boiler. When the injectors are on they force water at above boiler pressure past the clacks; when the injectors are off the boiler pressure forces the clacks back onto their seating - or it should do. Sometimes a clack could remain jammed open when the injector was shut off and this resulted in steam at high velocity escaping to the atmosphere via the injector water overflow pipe. The only course of action was to climb onto the boiler armed with a coal pick and spanner. The practice of hitting the clackbox casting with a coal pick was frowned upon in case it split, which would cause a rapid escape of steam from the boiler, and the total failure of the loco. However, it often did the trick and closed the clack. Many clackboxes were fitted with a square-ended spindle which could be screwed down (if you were lucky) so forcing the clacks onto their seat, hence the spanner. Dave managed this difficult job successfully, after which the driver would not hear a word said against him!

Not long before passing out to drive in 1967, Dave was sometimes teamed with Horace Plant, firing or riding as second man, as the traction dictated. Horace had definite views on certain types of diesel. They once worked the "Pines Express" between Birmingham and Oxford. As they approached the city, there waiting at the head of the return train was a Western Region diesel hydraulic "Warship". They were powerful but very noisy and hot. Horace immediately said, "You're driving back!"

By 1967, Jim Male of Wolverhampton Oxley had graduated from firing local pick-up goods, passing through the links fairly quickly to work both freight and passenger trains to such places as Banbury, Crewe, Oxford and Bristol, with some lodging turns to Paddington. He was firing on most types of main line locos, from Kings down to Manors, exactly what he had dreamed of doing as a 14 year old in 1946, but then the introduction of dmus caused job losses at Wolverhampton. Many men were downgraded, others were transferred to Bescot. Stafford Road shed closed in 1963, followed by the workshop in 1964 and Bushbury shed in 1965. Oxley shed closed in 1967. During this difficult period when so many jobs were lost, Jim became a passed fireman (ie; qualified to drive) in 1961 and a driver in his own right in 1965. He was made redundant when Oxley closed, at a time when he had, *"a wife, two children and a mortgage - where do you go from there?"*

A type of locomotive once familiar in the Midlands and elsewhere, an immaculate Class 25, No. 25 041, with a northbound coal train on the Camp Hill line on 9th November 1976. It is passing the site of Moseley station and emerging from Moseley tunnel, structurally unnecessary but built to pacify the parish church authorities. An Act of 1865 gave permission for the railway to open the tunnel out. The parish church of St.Mary is off camera to the right, the spire belongs to the local Baptist church.

(Michael Mensing)

He transferred to Bescot, with about twenty others from Oxley, all of whom had to be re-trained. They had to learn how to drive diesel and electric main line locos, and acquire the route knowledge that went with it - to Euston, Liverpool, Manchester, Warrington, Sheffield, etc. It was to be 1982 before any vacancies occurred at High Level, and Jim could return to Wolverhampton ....

There were, of course, some incidents which were unexpected and some situations which never featured in the rule book. Ray Churchill recalls being in charge of a Class 08 diesel shunter in Bescot yard. It was a busy night, with about twenty trains needing to be hump shunted and sorted. Ray was at the controls - in an 08 the control panel was nicknamed 'the piano' - but his loco was in need of maintenance, growling and vibrating badly. This caused the doors on the front of the piano to keep coming open, exposing the main motor contacts to the naked eye. If these part with a lot of current across them there is a loud bang and a flash like lightning. Having split the train, the shunter came to sit in the cab for a few minutes. When Ray attempted to restart the 08, there was a surge of power beyond the safe limit of 800amps. This caused the overload relay to operate and open the motor contacts. To regain power you had to close the power handle and start again. Some 08s - and this was one - would reset with the power handle still on, even though they were not supposed to. There would then be a whole series of bangs and flashes, with the loco bucking like a bronco. When the loud and colourful display from the piano was finally complete Ray looked round - the door was open, the seat was empty, the shunter had fled and was not seen for the remainder of the night!

The cab of a diesel loco gave former steam crews vastly increased visibility, but also placed them at greater risk from missiles. An alternative destination for training runs was Banbury, which could be approached at speed. As Ray slowed for the stop with a Class 24 'Fruit Machine', but still travelling at 70mph, there was a loud "Whump!" on the front of the cab. At Banbury shed the loco was checked for damage. There was none but there, sitting on the handrail, was an owl, alive and well, with just a speck of blood visible at the side of his beak. As several men gathered and gawped in disbelief he took off, flew between them and wheeled away over the coaling plant.

Ever since railways began, some railwaymen have always proved more than capable of creating their own interesting diversions. I was told the story, corroborated by two men who prefer to remain anonymous, of a certain Bescot driver who was an expert with the fog detonators. In one of his many escapades, about 1955, his train was standing at signals at Bridgeman Place, Walsall, waiting for the fast Sheffield freight to pass through. The guard was becoming impatient, it was the end of their shift and they were only going to Walsall yard. He left his van for the box. There followed a frank exchange of views between guard and signalman, during which time the driver stealthily placed as many detonators as possible on the track. After the Sheffield freight had passed, the train moved away. The driver somehow managed to keep an innocent expression on his face as explosions filled the air. It was about 2am. Many local people woke in alarm and a number of police were soon on the scene, thinking it may have been an explosion at the nearby gasworks .....

That driver was lucky, not so one of the foremen at Stourbridge shed. As late as the 1950s, lads who left school at 15 began a career on the railway in largely nineteenth century working conditions, even though this was the dawn of the diesel era. Stourbridge had its batch of 'call-up lads', who had to meet under the town clock in the middle of the night. They had lists of train crew who would need waking for the early shift, the first of them at 3am. Cycling in pairs to every home in turn, they woke each man by tapping at his bedroom window with the end of a long pole. A shed foreman used to delight in scaring the wits out of them, especially if they were new. As they cycled up one particularly dark hill he would approach downhill on his bike, swiftly, silently and without lamps, hurtling between them, cackling loudly afterwards. One night, what he took to be cycle lamps were actually the sidelights of a parked car, causing him an unscheduled stay in hospital .....

Alongside these ancient rituals, which no doubt occurred in various forms throughout the country, the railway was at last beginning to modernise. Experience with diesel traction was still very limited but that was about to change. There were stirrings even before the Modernisation Plan was published. As early as July 1952 the "Railway Magazine" reported trial running of an experimental lightweight diesel train between Marylebone and Princes Risborough. This was not the prototype 'Derby Lightweight' dmu but a different animal altogether, the so-called 'Flying Brick'. F.W.Shuttleworth's photograph was taken in August 1953, during a week's trial running on the Snow Hill-Wolverhampton line. Its statistics suggest that this was not a robust train and would have proved an unworthy

Was this the first occasion on which passengers were known as customers?

(F.W. Shuttleworth collection)

and dismal successor to local steam services if production models had ever been built. Each vehicle had just four wheels, which would have given an interestingly turbulent ride, as on the more recent Pacers. The AEC six-cylinder engines were identical to those of a London Transport Green Line bus. Top speed was a pathetic 45mph. Ventilation was bracing and the provision of entrance doors, just the minimum possible of two per vehicle, was not designed for a busy or even a semi-quiet train. This diesel, had two powered units, one with a guard's compartment, and a trailer car inbetween. Total weight was 39.7 tons, seating capacity was 129.

Fortunately it was only a matter of months (January 1953) before the "Railway Magazine" was holding out the prospect of something much more substantial than the 'brick' - *"British Railways are to introduce multiple-unit diesel trains for passenger traffic. With the approval of the British Transport Commission, the Railway Executive is undertaking an immediate*

first expenditure of up to £500,000 on this programme. This is the first practical step in the policy of using lightweight diesel units wherever suitable to reinforce or replace steam services."

These were the famous Derby Lightweight units, which gave reliable service for decades on local lines throughout the country, starting on the Leeds-Bradford line in June 1954. They began regular service in the West Midlands, between New Street and Lichfield, in March 1956, but there were two interesting curtain raisers before that - one diesel, one steam.

Every year the British Industries Fair (BIF) was held at Olympia and at Castle Bromwich, in its hall alongside the main line, near the station. It was a valuable weapon in the constant drive to increase exports. The Conservative Chancellor, R.A.Butler, sent a message of support to the fair in its 40th year, 1955, in which he highlighted the great variety of products on display, *"from excavating machinery to dinner services, from turbines to costume jewellery, from mobile cranes to nail*

Not so much a heritage dmu, more a 'pre-heritage' dmu. This was an experimental three-car railbus, nick-named the 'Flying Brick'. Each car had skirted sides and four wheels. The yellow livery of the roof and upper body was separated from the blue of the lower half by a red waistband. There was no destination blind, the driver sat in a half-width cab, ventilation was bracing and - a potentially dangerous design fault - each car side had only one single-width door. The set is seen leaving Priestfield with the 7.10pm from Snow Hill to Wolverhampton (LL) on 18th August 1953. It ran on this route for a week and passengers were issued with a questionnaire. The Worcester line is on the right. The present day Priestfield Metro stop is on straight track, a few metres nearer Wolverhampton. (F.W.Shuttleworth)

An early Derby lightweight dmu on the first special diesel shuttle service between New Street and Castle Bromwich, for the British Industries Fair, 29th April 1954. The train carries a customised headboard and the station sign is in four languages.

(courtesy of Birmingham Post & Mail)

scissors. And alongside our traditional products are our newest; things like synthetic fibres and nucleonic (sic) instruments. I wish the BIF all success in demonstrating to the world the abounding strength and vitality of our industry."

The "Birmingham Post" (2nd May 1955) added, *"Visitors who travel to the BIF by rail from New Street will have a foretaste of the new diesel train service which British Railways plan to introduce shortly on the Sutton Coldfield line. For the railways are using the BIF as a shop window for their new service. A diesel train will make nine journeys a day in each direction between Birmingham and Castle Bromwich. Steam trains will run the normal 12-minute service during the Fair."* The same paper's photograph shows the train at Castle Bromwich after its first trip on 29th April 1955. The six-car train consisted of Derby Lightweight units, complete with special roofboards. Notice the bowler hat and the station sign in no fewer than four languages. What cannot be seen is the long permanent way slack on the approach to Castle Bromwich, which prevented the new dmus from really 'stretching their legs' for the duration of the fair! For the fifty weeks of the year in which the fair was not held, Castle Bromwich was served by Leicester and Sutton Park line local trains. The station closed in 1968, just *after* construction of the adjacent large housing estate at Castle Vale had begun. The BIF exhibition hall was demolished to make way for it, as was the former Castle Bromwich aerodrome from where, before the war, more adventurous travellers could fly to Cardiff in a Great Western Air Services plane, which had a seating capacity of eight.

Doubtless today's inhabitants of Castle Vale would welcome the return of a train service. Residents of well-healed Sutton Coldfield never lost their's. The population of this royal borough more than doubled between the 1931 and 1951 censuses - from 23,000 to 47,000 - but the train service did not improve to match. Sutton was home to many professional people who worked in Birmingham so, despite rather than because of the train service, this was the busiest local line in the area. In the morning peak the 8.18am from Four Oaks ran fast south of Wylde Green, except for the time-consuming ticket stop at Vauxhall. An all-stations service left Four Oaks ten minutes later, after which there was a gap of over two hours. The evening peak was better, with departures from New Street at 5.17, 5.27, 5.42 and 6.02, but in both directions there were long gaps in the middle of the day and in the evening. There were no departures from New Street between 8.50am and 12.10pm. In 1954, with diesels just over the horizon, the steam service was transformed. The trains became push-pull, or 'motor trains', in which the loco could push its two carriages from the rear, eliminating run round at journey's end. When in this mode the fireman stayed in the cab and the driver drove from the specially adapted leading coach by means of various mechanical linkages between his cab and the loco. This was a long and basic system of transmission, but it had worked well since the early years of the century on branch line motor trains throughout the country. Trains now ran between New Street and Sutton Coldfield (rapidly extended to Four Oaks) at regular intervals - once every hour. The Walsall and Harborne lines had operated at regular intervals since the beginning of the century, only to suffer from cut backs during the First World War. An hourly clock face local train service was a novelty not seen for many years. It was a success, with over 750,000 people using the line in 1955. When the service was completely dieselised without ceremony, on 5th March 1956, it was improved further. Off peak trains were now half-hourly between Birmingham and Four Oaks, and hourly to Lichfield City. The peak hour service remained essentially the same as in steam days, although trains were marginally faster. They were strengthened as traffic increased, with 4 two-car sets or 3 three-car sets able to run

together. For a while in the early 1960s loco-hauled stock was used on some of the busiest trains.

The original two-car Derby Lightweights entered service before the Modernisation Plan was published. They were a logical development, in substance if not in style, of the Great Western diesel railcars, the first of which was built in 1933. The GWR ordered 20 two-car sets in 1939. They were delivered during the early part of the war and immediately had to cope with gross overcrowding, especially on the Snow Hill-Cardiff run, where there was at first just one daily working each way, with an ordinary carriage sandwiched between the two power cars. It was a difficult way to enter the world, but the diesel multiple unit was born.

The external dimensions of the Lightweights were based on those of the new Standard British Railways (Mark I) corridor coach. Each car was 57 feet long. Power was provided by bus type 150bhp diesel engines which generated a top speed of 62mph. Most passenger carriages in service in 1954 weighed at least 30 tons; the Lightweight power cars were 27 tons, trailer cars were just 21 tons. Each two-car set had a guard's van, a toilet and (with small variations) seating capacity for 16 first and 114 third class passengers. Third class was re-designated second class after the first dmus entered service. Corridor connections on local trains were almost unheard of in steam days, causing the "Railway Magazine" (July 1954) to comment that in the Lightweights, *"the two vehicles of each unit intercommunicate through a vestibule type corridor connection similar to that obtaining in long-distance passenger stock"*. First class seats were arranged in facing pairs on either side of the gangway. In 3rd class the aisle was off-centre, two seats on one side, three on the other, all facing the cab. *"To reduce condensation and noise the whole of the inside structure and the underside of the floor is sprayed with asbestos"*. One novel feature, used in publicity at the time, was the clear view of the line ahead from the passenger saloon via the driver's cab. The windows at the rear of his cab were almost as large as those at the front, with blinds which he could let down at night to cut out the light from behind, although the 'headlights' were minimal on all first generation dmus, intended mainly for identification by signalmen.

The Modernisation Plan was preceeded by a report published by a committee of senior members of the British Transport Commission, aimed at securing a large financial investment in a modern railway system. The committee issued its report in April 1953, but it had only been formed at the beginning of that year. The document contained many vague platitudes. It was full of nice round figures but short on substance - sure signs that it was cobbled together too quickly. It sought investment of £500 million, of which £17 million was to be spent on the "Introduction of diesel rail-cars" and £160 million on electrification. Although not acted upon directly, this report was important in further helping to persuade the government that the railways were in need of considerable investment.

The Modernisation Plan itself was drawn up by a BTC Planning Committee, chaired by Daril Watson, which presented its proposals to the Minister of Transport, John Boyd-Carpenter, in December 1954. An amended public document was published the following month. Investment spending was to be £1,240 million over 15 years but, as the Commission recognised in its Annual Report for 1954, *£600 million would in any event have had to be spent over the period of the Plan merely to maintain the existing equipment"*. A seemingly colossal sum was suddenly not that big; over 15 years it would work out at £42 million per year on new investment at 1954 prices, with no allowance for inflation.

The 1953 report had made no provision for main line diesel locomotives, as all main lines of any consequence were to have

The 10.32am Burton-New St, (via Lichfield and Sutton), March 1956.   The loco is a member of British Railways' smallest class of Standard tender engines, designed for branch line use. 2-6-0 No.78038 (2MT) was shedded at Bescot (3A) and was deputising for a Burton 4-4-0. Chester Road had a lady porter.   *(Peter Myatt)*

The first day of dieselised commuter travel on the Birmingham-Lichfield line, 5th March 1956.   *(courtesy of Birmingham Post & Mail)*

been electrified. The Modernisation Plan shifted the emphasis. £185 million was to be spent on main line electrification and £150 million on dieselisation, of which £125 million was for locomotives, the remainder for dmus. This move away from a large scale and purposeful rolling programme of electrification was a huge mistake. The railway system, locally and nationally, still bears the scars.

The Plan, warmly welcomed by the government at first, subsequently stuttered and faltered before being swept away by the Beeching Report of 1963. Meanwhile, having been starved of meaningful investment since before the war, railway management of 1955 were Ready to Spend! However, they had forgotten the art of spending wisely, were intoxicated by the prospect of a limitless supply of shiny new technology and soon found themselves writing big cheques for large numbers of production locomotives before many of their prototypes had proved their trackworthiness. Many classes of diesel locomotives built as a result of the Plan were successful; too many were not. A few diesel classes were virtually stillborn, extinct almost as soon as the steam types they were meant to replace.

The Modernisation Plan rightly made no provision for any more steam traction. However, loco building was continuing, contracts had to be honoured and the new Standard classes were performing well. It was envisaged that they would have a useful life of at least twenty years (ie; until about 1975) but in the event they were scrapped with indecent haste, cut up in their prime.

The major success story of the Plan, nationally and locally, was that of the diesel multiple unit. They lacked glamour, but were reliable, hard-working and less expensive than the steam they replaced. They transformed local and middle distance services, saving many from closure or a long decline. (The first two closures of any note in the West Midlands after 1955 were of lines which were never worked by dmus; Wolverhampton-Stourbridge Junction and Old Hill-Dudley.) When new they brought many more people onto the railway. The 750,000 passengers who used the Sutton Coldfield line during 1955 had increased to almost 1½ million by 1959. In old age, during the 1980s, at a time when the railways were once again starved of realistic levels of investment, they did not just maintain the service. On most lines out of Birmingham passenger numbers were rising and service levels were expanding to meet the demand. The 'heritage' units were worked harder than ever before. They operated all the services out of the new Snow Hill when it opened in 1987. Right until its absurdly overdue electrification, which finally began in 1990, the four-trains-an-hour Cross City route was probably the busiest diesel-operated local line in the world. It would be hard to overestimate the value of the humble dmu.

The Derby Lightweights were successful pioneers, soon joined by other types built as a result of the Modernisation Plan. Metro-Cammell, of Birmingham, had built no fewer than 798 dmus by the end of 1959. The late 1950s witnessed a boom in rolling stock construction, especially dmus. National figures for the total number of dmus built for British Railways between 1954 and 1962 are as follows:- 34 (1954), 111 (55), 275 (56), 904 (57), 1070 (58), 832 (59), 575 (60), 183 (61) and 93 (1962).

The Class 101 Metro-Cammell lightweight units (26.5 ton power cars; 25 ton trailers) differed in appearance from the Derby Lightweights. The top of each cab end sloped back slightly and its windows were smaller, as were those in the passenger saloons. The continuous roof gutter was missing, replaced by a short gutter above each entrance door. As with the Derby vehicles, each power car was provided with two 150bhp AEC bus type diesel engines. When new they were painted a dark green, known officially by the inspired title of Mutliple Unit Green;

known to some steam-loving boys of the day as 'greenslime'. The 101s were lined, like other types, in cream, with the addition of a third line parallel with the base of the window vents. They gave many years' service in the West Midlands, beginning on the ex-LMS lines making later forays onto the ex-Great Western. There are no longer any in the area but the last few survivors are still (1998) operational in the Glasgow area. One set, restored to its original livery, is based at Chester for the summer service on the Llandudno Junction-Blaenau Ffestiniog line.

Three other types of easily distinguishable dmu were once widespread in the West Midlands. The Park Royal units were similar to the Derby Lightweights but the saloon behind the cab was longer, needing three side windows rather than two. Only twenty two-car sets were built by Park Royal, at their Stockport works, in 1957. Certain components were none standard, so it made sense to allocate them collectively - when new they were all based at Ryecroft. The Gloucester Railway Carriage & Wagon units (Class 100) had similar vital statistics to the Derby Lightweights and Metro-Cammells. Their distinguishing feature was the cab end, with minimal styling, which gave them an unfinished appearance.

Most Western Region local services were operated by High Density units, supplied by a variety of builders from 1957. Virtually identical in appearance these were designated Class 116 (Derby), 117 (Pressed Steel) and 118 (Birmingham Railway Carriage & Wagon Co.Ltd.). At first they were non-corridor, with internal partitions between smoking and non-smoking sections. These were later removed and corridors added, giving all passengers access to the toilet. This also improved the guard's ability to reach passengers who had boarded at unstaffed stations. Unlike other units described so far, provision of external doors was generous, one for each pair of facing seats. They were also heavier, at 35.5 tons per motor car and 28.5 tons per trailer, and therefore a little more sluggish, although superior to the steam they supplanted. With the passage of time they ceased to be confined to the Western Region. These were the units that struggled so valiantly, despite extreme old age and a chronic lack of spare parts, to keep the Cross City Line going before the handover to electrics began in 1992. Classes 122 and 123 were single unit variations, the so-called 'bubble cars', which operated the last services out of Snow Hill before closure in 1972 and also ran the Town Car at Stourbridge for many years after that.

Birmingham's Western Region dmus were based at Tyseley, an early twentieth century steam shed which geared up for the new arrivals during 1956 - *"Special facilities include a storage depot to supply diesel fuel to trains at 130 gallons a minute. A maintenance building will accommodate three three-car sets; it will have a reinforced-concrete barrel vault roof and, for ready access to under-floor engines, tracks raised above general floor level on concrete supports and a longitudinal pit between each of the three tracks."* (Railway Magazine).

All this investment was reaping dividends. When Sir Brian Robertson, Chairman of the British Transport Commission, spoke in Birmingham on 1st May 1959 about plans for rebuilding New Street station, he also revealed figures about the dmus - *"Passengers using the diesel suburban services run by the London Midland Region in the area rose by over 31,000 in January this year, compared with the same month last year."*

By 1960 most local services, especially on the Western Region, had been completely dieselised (except for a few hard-pressed peak workings) and were running to a regular interval time-table. They can be summarised as follows -

A pair of the distinctive and once familiar 3-car Swindon 'Cross Country' dmus passing Bordesley station with the 3.10pm (SX) from Carmarthen via Chepstow to Snow Hill (arr.8.12pm). Each passenger saloon had two heaters, not one for each side, as was normal, but one for the front and one for the back, which tended to make the cars either too hot or too cool. Bordersley yard is beyond the Camp Hill line bridge. 20th July 1961. *(Michael Mensing)*

London Midland Region:
New Street - Four Oaks (1/2hourly) and Lichfield City (hourly)
New Street - Walsall and Rugeley Trent Valley (hourly)
New Street - Redditch (hourly)
Wolverhampton - Walsall (hourly) and Burton via Lichfield City (two-hourly)
Walsall - Dudley (hourly)

Western Region:
One train per hour in each direction -
Wellington - Wolverhampton LL - Snow Hill - Lapworth
Moor Street - Leamington Spa
Dudley - Great Bridge - Snow Hill *
(Bewdley SO) - Kidderminster - Snow Hill
Moor Street - Henley - Stratford
* British Railways may have been in existence since 1948, but these Western Region trains ran through the ex-LMS station at Dudley Port (Low Level) without stopping!

All these Western Region local services became regular interval on the same day, 17th June 1957.
Sample day return fares from Birmingham Snow Hill were Shirley 1/6d (7p), Stratford or Leamington 5/6d (27p), Solihull 2/1d (10p), Wednesbury 1/9d (8p), Wolverhampton 3/4d (16p).

Western Region longer distance dmus entered service on 10th May 1958. Known as Cross Country units, with low density seating and mini-buffets, they provided a fast efficient link between Birmingham and South Wales, just as their Great Western predecessors had done over twenty years earlier. In the summer of 1960 these Swindon-built sets left Snow Hill (Mon-Fri) for Cardiff via Stourbridge, Worcester and Hereford at 08.00, 10.00, 12.00, 13.00, 17.40 and 20.05. Journey time averaged 3 hours 15 minutes. They also provided a service to Swansea via Stratford, Cheltenham, Chepstow and Cardiff, leaving Snow Hill at 08.10, 12.25 and 17.05, the first two working through to Carmarthen. These three-car sets, Class 120, were built between 1958 and 1961. The motor cars weighed 36 tons, the trailers 31 tons. In later years, after Snow Hill closed to main line traffic in 1967, they were to be seen on New Street services to Hereford, Leicester and East Anglia. They could seat 18 first and 144 second class passengers in considerable comfort. Internal decor was enlivened by curtains and distinctive oval mirrors. Unfortunately, none of these units escaped the cutter's torch.

The Western Region began withdrawing the "King" Class steam locos early in 1962. All had gone by the end of the year. These magnificent beasts, thirty in number, had been the mainstay of the Paddington-Bristol and Paddington-Wolverhampton services since the late 1920s. Wolverhampton Stafford Road was normally home to about six members of the class. At least seven "Kings" were awaiting their fate when the accompanying photograph was taken at Stafford Road on Sunday 9th September 1962, by which date only four members of the class were still in active service. The following day saw full dieselisation of the Wolverhampton-Paddington main line. The "Birmingham Evening Mail" outlined the events which marked the occasion under the headline –

The Western Region still masqueraded as the Great Western Railway - which always did things differently - even into the diesel era. This resulted in its own series of diesel hydraulic main line locomotives which flourished for a few brief years. Class 52 D1005 "Western Venturer" stands on the centre road at Wolverhampton Low Level waiting, with strengthening coaches, to take over the up "Cambrian Coast Express", 27th August 1962. These locos had good strong engines, a comfortable ride and swift acceleration. They could easily keep time with the accelerated Paddington expresses. *(Michael Mensing)*

"A civic send off for Snow Hill's faster diesel trains".

"The Lord Mayor of Birmingham waved his green flag and the Alderman at the controls sent the diesel loco speeding on its way to London. That was how the new faster diesel services between Birmingham and London were inaugurated at Snow Hill.

The Lord Mayor, Alderman Ernest Horton, was merely acting as the guard. He blew his whistle, nipped smartly into the guard's van and then took his seat in a first class compartment. But the Alderman had to stay at the controls of the chocolate coloured "Western King" locomotive. For Alderman W.S.Jones, of Shrewsbury Borough Council, this was just another day's work. He has been driving locomotives for 25 years. (The train) left on time at 8.20. It was the start of the All Change day on British Railways.

Timetables have been reorganised by the speedier London to Birmingham services and the switch of some trains from Snow Hill to New Street. The two fastest trains on the inter-city run are now the 9am and 2.10pm Paddington to Snow Hill, both scheduled to do the trip in 1 hour 50 minutes. The fastest Snow Hill to Paddington trip is the 4pm, which is scheduled to do the journey in 1 hour 54 minutes.

Other changes today include the switch of two famous expresses.

The "Cornishman", which used to start from Wolverhampton and travel via Snow Hill, today started from Sheffield and travelled via New Street. The "Pines Express", from Manchester to Bournemouth, which used to run via Stafford, Wolverhampton and New Street, today began running through Market Drayton, Snow Hill, Oxford and Reading."

Cecil J. Allen, a railway author for over fifty years, was on board the 9am from Paddington on September 10th. In his regular column in "Modern Railways", 'Locomotive Running Past & Present' (November 1962) he related how D1038 "Western Sovereign" hauled its eight-coach 290 ton train into Snow Hill just 103 mins 50 secs after leaving Paddington.

Also with effect from September 10th, steam on local services out of Snow Hill was confined to a few of the lengthier peak hour trains, all of which were now made up entirely of corridor stock. Withdrawal of non-corridor suburban coaches resulted in the closure of Wolverhampton Low Level carriage shed.

Thus, by the autumn of 1962, the majority of trains that operated out of Snow Hill - local, cross country or main line - were less than six years old. Although the "Western" diesels were brand new in 1962, Snow Hill's most modern train had been running since September 1960.

Forlorn "Kings" at Wolverhampton Stafford Road, 20th September 1962. Nearest the camera is 6017 "King Edward IV". Only four members of the class remained on active service at this time. *(courtesy of Birmingham Post & Mail)*

2-6-0 No.6364 (ex-GW 4300 Class) approaching Tyseley with the 17.38 local from Snow Hill to Lapworth on 28th August 1964. This train loaded to ten carriages and with so many stops was difficult to work. After trying various classes of loco, 6364 established itself as favourite for the job.

(Robert Darlaston)

Western Blue

Monday 12th September 1960 was the first day of the 1960-61 winter time-table. The "Inter-City", still steam-hauled, left Paddington at 9am, arriving at Snow Hill at 11.13 and Wolverhampton at 11.40. The up service left Wolverhampton at 4.35pm, Snow Hill at 5pm and arrived at Paddington at 7.15pm, having stopped additionally at Leamington Spa. Speed had slipped a little since 1953. The "Cornishman" left Wolverhampton at 9am, called at Bilston, Wednesbury and West Bromwich before Snow Hill (9.40) then proceeded via Stratford and Bristol to Penzance (arr.5.55pm). The Kidderminster portion of the "Cathedrals Express" left at 8.20am and joined the main train at Worcester Shrub Hill, which arrived in Paddington at 11.25am. All these schedules are of historic interest; none is important when set alongside a completely new train that entered service on the same day. This was a diesel multiple unit with a difference, the "Birmingham Pullman".

As part of the Modernisation Plan, five Pullman diesel multiple unit train sets were ordered from Metro-Cammell of Birmingham. There were two six-car trains, for first class passengers only, which entered service between St.Pancras and Manchester via Derby in 1959. This was the "Midland Pullman", so-called only because it used the main line of the former Midland Railway. Three eight-car sets followed, with first and second class accommodation. They were to provide a quality business service between Paddington and Bristol, Paddington, Cardiff and Swansea, and Paddington, Snow Hill and Wolverhampton, the "Birmingham Pullman".

Two full sized mock-ups of the cab were built at Saltley, to make final decisions on its aerodynamic shape and to fine tune the position of the controls. The eight-car trains had seating for 108 first and 120 second class passengers. All seats could be reserved. There were two kitchen cars and much was made of the fact that all passengers could be served meals at their seats. As the BR leaflet stated, *The vehicles are of the saloon, centre vestibule type and special consideration has been given to the exterior styling and to the interior decor. Meals and refreshments will be served throughout the trains, to the traditional high Pullman standards.*

The trains were powered by two 1,000 horse power engines, each coupled directly to a main generator. Engine and generator were housed on special mountings in an effort to eliminate vibration. Each power car also incorporated a driving cab, guard's compartment and a small saloon for 18 passengers. The fuel tanks had a capacity of 1,000 gallons and the weight of an eight car train was 364 tons.

The design of the Blue Pullman was a great leap forward, with a number of important innovations. It rode on bogies which had been specially developed for a high quality smooth ride yet which would need little maintenance - at least that was the intention! The underframes were of the box girder type and the metal shell of the train consisted of a strong corrosion resistant steel. Sections were joined by means of spot welding. Corridor connections were wider than on conventional stock. They were also airtight because this was the first train in Britain to be fully air-conditioned. The passenger saloons were insulated all-round against heat and sound. The floor 'floated' on special rubber pads.

Every attention was paid to the comfort of the passengers. All the deeply-padded seats had armrests, those in first class could be reclined and moved nearer to or further from their tables. The aisle in both first and second class was off-centre, with seats and tables for four on one side, two on the other. The attendant was summoned by means of a bell push under each window, which was framed in aluminium and double glazed, with a Venetian blind between the glazing. The guard could communicate with passengers via a public address system; he could also talk with the driver by a private link described as a 'Loudaphone' (sic).

The passenger saloons were carpeted, and decorated in a variety of soft colours, blues or reds predominating, even on the mini-tiles on the floor of each toilet. The lighting was carefully thought out, with a continuous centre roof strip for maximum visibility and softer strips under the luggage racks to eliminate harshness. Each table had an individual lamp. The partitions were of polished rosewood, into which were inlaid attractive semi-abstract murals. Externally the Pullmans were finished in a colour described as Nanking blue, after the blue porcelain produced in that Chinese city. The window surrounds were white.

The Pullmans' first running trials took place on the Sutton Park line which was ideal for several reasons. It was near to Metro-Cammell; it saw comparatively few freight trains during the day and even fewer passenger trains; there were long stretches passed for fast running up to 90mph, including a recently laid section of continuous welded rail - one of the first in the country. A full colour transfer of the distinctive Pullman crest was applied to each cab end after the first running trials. The driver wore a distinctive white uniform and cap, whereas other diesel drivers still wore the same uniform as steam train crew until 1964.

The Birmingham Pullman also served Wolverhampton, Solihull and Leamington. The morning up and evening down services, despite the top speed of 90mph, still took 2 hours 5 minutes between Paddington and Snow Hill. The lunchtime working, which left Paddington at 12.10pm, omitted the Solihull stop and stopped short at Snow Hill, which it reached in 1 hour 55 minutes. The second class Pullman return fare between Snow Hill and Paddington was 47 shillings (£2.35), rising to £2.60 from Wolverhampton, but a modest £1.85 from Leamington and £2.20 from Solihull. The eight-car Birmingham Pullman was stabled at Tyseley but regularly serviced at Derby overnight, sometimes hauled there by a Black Five, a Standard 9F or any other locomotive to hand.

For a few years the Birmingham Pullman was easily the most prestigious and comfortable train on the line. However, it was not without its problems, or its indignities. The midday working on 9th February 1962, for example, was full of unwanted incident, according to a report in the April "Railway Magazine" by one of the luckless passengers, who also had an eventful return journey. The Pullman failed in Paddington station, having travelled roughly three feet towards Birmingham. Passengers were transferred to the South Wales set, which had just arrived from Cardiff. This train left at 10.35am, 25 minutes late. It made up about 15 minutes lost time en route, only to be held at Bordesley for half an hour by a failed diesel on a freight train in Snow Hill tunnel. Arrival was 45 minutes late. The correspondent returned on the 5pm "Inter-City", with 'twelve on' (390 tons) behind 6016 "King Edward V", which expired with smokebox trouble on the through line at Beaconsfield, away from the platforms. After a 40 minute wait, help appeared in the unlikely guise of 0-6-0 pannier tank No.5766, which deposited the King in a nearby siding and then - no doubt with its 4 foot 7 inch driving wheels flailing in a demented fashion - hauled the train to Paddington, taking just 29 minutes for the 22 miles!

The Blue Pullmans were soon overtaken by events. Electrification of the West Coast Main Line caused the "Midland Pullman" sets to be placed in store in 1966 and replaced by the "Manchester Pullman" from Euston, with new electric locomotives and Mark II Pullman cars. The "Birmingham Pullman" was withdrawn the following year when main line electric trains reached New Street. When it left Snow Hill for the last time on Friday 3rd March 1967, it still carried its original

The "Blue Pullman" enters Birmingham Snow Hill with the 12.10pm from Paddington, 28th March 1961. The train will terminate here and depart for Paddington from the same platform   *(Michael Mensing)*

livery. It then became a spare set. In 1968 all sets were repainted in standard rail blue and grey - with colours reversed compared to non-Pullman stock - and the cabs were given an all yellow end. All the sets were withdrawn by 1973; none was preserved.

They had many years' potential service remaining but two factors caused their early demise. The Schlieren pattern bogies, specially developed for a smooth ride, proved difficult to maintain. They were suited to the characteristics of main line track in Germany, which already had a considerable amount of continuous welded rail, rather than British permanent way, which did not. To the layman this may seem strange, but any motorist will know the different 'feel' of a concrete road surface compared to tar; any tennis player can distinguish between the characteristics of a clay and a grass court and will adapt his game accordingly. But the maintenance of the Schlieren bogies did not take into account the necessity for such fine tuning and the ride became increasingly rough, with no cure in sight. The respected railway author O.S.Nock reserved some harsh words for them in his regular column in "Railway Magazine", describing the ride (August 1963) as *"purgatorial"* with a *"peculiar shuddering effect"*. Later, the Pullmans were marketed as suitable for football excursions, as they never ran in normal service at weekends. The Birmingham set was hired on at least two occasions. It ran from Walsall to Norwich for an FA cup tie on 12th February 1966 and from Coventry to Liverpool three weeks later. I have no information as to what the fans thought of the ride!

The second factor concerned the all-round improvement in long distance rail travel. The Pullmans were always meant as premium trains but as new diesel and electric main line locomotives entered service, ordinary long distance trains improved dramatically in speed and frequency. The new Mark II coaches added to passengers' comfort. There was no longer any reason to keep what had become expensive non-standard trains. However, from the lessons learnt during the Blue Pullman years there emerged the ultimate diesel multiple unit - the High Speed Train.

A pre-electric semi-fast working for what would later be known as 'heritage' dmus. These Class 104 units were built by Birmingham Railway Carriage & Wagon Co. and they are very close to their birthplace as they pass Smethwick Rolfe Street with the Birmingham New St.-Manchester Piccadilly via Stoke on Sunday 2nd February 1964.   (*Michael Mensing*)

Made in Birmingham

In a sense much of this section has already been written. Metro-Cammell built far more Modernisation Plan dmus than any other company, not to mention the Blue Pullman sets (and 44 Pullman coaches for the East Coast Main Line in 1960). These were not their only important orders during the period covered by this book, neither was Metro-Cammell Birmingham's only train maker.

The Birmingham Railway Carriage & Wagon Co. (BRCW) also produced a wide range of rolling stock for the domestic and overseas market. Its factory straddled the Birmingham/Smethwick boundary, west of Handsworth & Smethwick station. After the war, during which the works had been given over mainly to the production of tanks, BRCW produced corridor coaches for the Southern and LNER, only to deliver them, early in 1948, to the infant British Railways. 1949-51 was a busy period for the construction of London Underground stock, involving 89 non-driving motor cars of surface stock (R47) and 91 tube stock cars. As peacetime conditions improved, some pre-war luxuries were reinstated and in 1951 BRCW completed an order for seven Pullman cars for use on the "Golden Arrow".

Probably the most important post-war order received by BRCW was for Mark I coaches. No fewer than 713 such vehicles of all types, including two experimental open saloons of 1957, were built here between 1953 and 1961. As the Modernisation Plan took effect, Class 104 and 118 dmus were also built at Smethwick, along with ninety-eight Class 26 and sixty-nine Class 27 locos, all delivered between 1959 and 1962. New ground was

broken in 1959 with the construction of E3001, the first 25Kv electric loco in the country, built for the West Coast Main Line. There were twenty-five such locos in the first batch, costing what was then a hefty £70,000 each and later designated Class 81. The rich variety of overseas orders included twelve diesel locos for Ireland (1956), eleven steamlined dmus for Egypt (1951), a special saloon for the Governor of Nigeria, which was still a British colony (1955) and sheep wagons for New Zealand (1951). Suburban electric multiple units were built for South Africa in 1958; their third class interiors were spartan in the extreme.

At the end of 1959 BRCW began construction of an experimental lightweight Class 4 diesel electric locomotive. The emphasis was on high power and low weight. It was light, 19 tons for each of six axles (114 tons) and in trials early in 1962 is said to have exceeded 100 mph. It hauled a test train of twenty coaches up the Lickey Incline unaided, from a standing start! This was the white liveried D0260 "Lion", built speculatively in the hope of attracting orders. Unfortunately there was none, either from British Railways or overseas, so it was withdrawn in October 1963 and broken up two years later. At a time of over capacity and shortening order books, "Lion" was an unsuccessful bid by BRCW to stay in the railway construction industry. In its final full year, 1962, BRCW made a profit of £370,000 and paid a dividend of 10%. Rather than risk sinking into oblivion, it ceased production but rented out the factory space to other businesses. The new holding company, The Birmingham Wagon Co., subsequently developed a wide range of business interests in property development, investment portfolios and industrial banking.

Class 81 electric loco No. 81 018, hauls a train of short wheelbase mineral wagons out of Walsall with a southbound coal train, 8th April 1977. Such Birmingham built machines were the first type of electric locos used on the West Coast Main Line. *(Michael Mensing)*

Near the beginning of the period covered by this book, BRCW shared an order with Metro-Cammell for some electric multiple units for British Railways, 92 for the Liverpool St.-Shenfield scheme and 8 for Manchester-Glossop. Power was by overhead collection at 1,500v, since converted to 25Kv. The accompanying photograph shows the interior of a Metro-Cammell built car for the Shenfield line, completed in 1949. There is a fascinating mix of features old and new. The seating can best be described as lurid and uncomfortable.

If the BRCW order for Mark I carriages was substantial, it was exceeded by Metro-Cammell, who built no fewer than 1,300 such vehicles. In the early 1950s the firm was one of the leaders in the change from steel to aluminium bodywork, with higher initial costs, but lower wear and maintenance and longer life. An early customer for aluminium-panelled stock was London Transport, which took delivery of 90 cars for the District Line (R49 stock) between 1951 and 1953. Each car weighed 28 tons, a saving of five tons over the steel-bodied equivalent, and one of the first to be delivered was displayed on the South Bank at the Festival of Britain. In 1957 Metro-Cammell built three prototype aluminium trains for the deep level tube lines. This resulted in a huge order for 1,039 such vehicles (over 140 complete trains), built between 1960 and 1964. Demand for the standard 16 ton mineral wagon continued unabated, with over 16,000 built at the works during the 1950s.

Alongside all this activity the export market flourished. During the 1950s orders included emus and electric locomotives for South Africa, coaches for Hong Kong and Egypt, diesel railcars for Jamaica (whose entire rail system has fallen into decay and recently closed), electric trains for India and locomotives for Pakistan and Ireland. A 1950 order was for thirty 3-car emus for the Central Railway of Brazil, to supplement their original Metro-Cammell stock of 1937. One picture which has found its way into company archives, reproduced here, is definitely not an official photograph, more like a family snapshot. Full of character, it shows one of the trains in Sao Paulo. The overcrowded toast-rack trams, heavy black car and palm tree all enliven the scene, as do the catenary and the colour light signalling - still rare on a British railway outside London in 1950.

In 1959 Metro-Cammell received an order for 35 electric locomotives for South African Railways' 3' 6" gauge system and the photograph - official this time - shows some units in the course of construction at one of the satellite factories, the Old Park Works, Wednesbury, during 1960. This was the last such order because after 1961 South Africa's trains were all built locally, but by a firm, Union Carriage & Wagon Co.Ltd., in which Metro-Cammell had a financial interest.

The more recent history of Metro-Cammell includes such landmarks as the Hong Kong Metro cars, the Tyne & Wear Metro, second generation diesel multiple units and Channel Tunnel trains. In addition, of course, there have been further large orders from what has become London Underground Limited. When waiting to leave an Underground train, a quick glance downwards by the doors will almost invariably reveal the words "Metro-Cammell" inscribed in the floor, a sure sign that, in this respect at least, Birmingham helps to keep London moving. All this must wait for the final volume of "A Century of Railways", when it will be seen that what is now GEC Alsthom Metro-Cammell Ltd. is as active as ever.

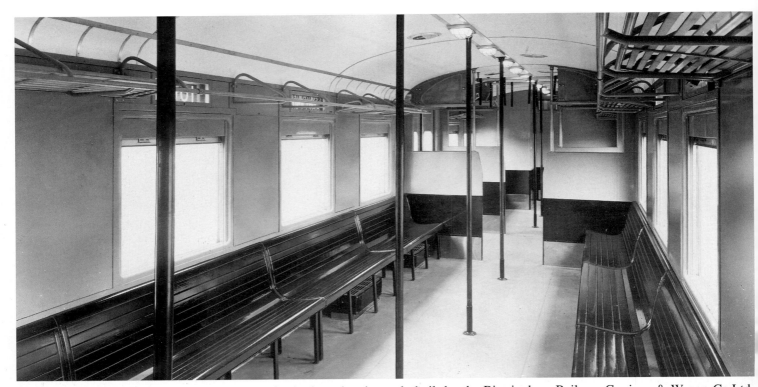

The spartan interior of a third class carriage of suburban electric stock, built by the Birmingham Railway Carriage & Wagon Co.Ltd. during 1958. The cars, to the SAR 3'6" gauge, could seat 60 passengers, with many more standees in uncomfortable crush loading conditions. These trains were for the lines serving Johannesburg and Soweto, in the days when passengers were rigidly segregated according to ethnic origin. It is a sobering thought that, having left the Birmingham builders, few white faces would ever gaze inside these vehicles again.
(courtesy of GEC Asthom Metro-Cammell)

Interior of a driving motor car for the Liverpool Street-Shenfield suburban electrification scheme, built by Metropolitan-Cammell in 1949. Features which seem old-fashioned to modern eyes, such as the swirling patterns on the fabric, string luggage racks and leather strap-handles, were mixed with more modern elements, notably the passenger operated sliding doors. At the far end, above the traditional three rural scenes, a diagrammatic map of the route is surmounted by the new British Railways totem.
(courtesy of GEC Asthom Metro-Cammell)

A Metro-Cammell built three-car electric multiple unit train, of the Central Railway of Brazil, bridges a main road in Sao Paulo. Thirty 3-car trains were ordered in 1937, with a repeat order for fifty more in 1950. These were the days when cars, robust as tanks, were almost always black. Most men wore hats, even when perched on the running boards of vintage toast rack tramcars.

(courtesy of GEC Alsthom Metro-Cammell)

Part of the production line of 35 type 5EI electric locomotives built for South African Railways at Metro Cammell's Old Park Works, Wednesbury, from an order placed on 21st May 1959.

(courtesy of GEC Alsthom Metro-Cammell)

[Diary : Notes : Stations : Freight : Beginnings & Endings]

DIARY

1963

January 1st - Significant Regional boundary changes mean that most ex-GW lines in the West Midlands are transferred to the London Midland Region, including the Paddington main line north of Banbury, the Bristol main line north of Stratford and the Stourbridge line as far south as Hartlebury.

March 27th - Beeching Report published.

September - Wolverhampton Stafford Road shed closed.

November 8th - Last freight train on the Harborne line.

1964

3rd January - Last day of Rubery-Northfield workmen's specials.

May 2nd - Last trains Dudley - Birmingham Snow Hill.

June 13th - Last trains on the 'Bumble Hole' line between Old Hill and Dudley.

July 4th - Last "Dudley Dasher" linking Dudley with Dudley Port; last Dudley-Walsall trains. These closures meant that Dudley became the first large town in the West Midlands without a rail passenger service (Dudley Port station is in Tipton and Sandwell & Dudley is in Oldbury!)

August 8th - Kidderminster shed closed.

September 27th - Bromsgrove shed closed.

1965

January 16th - Last day of service on Walsall-Wolverhampton, Walsall-Lichfield and Sutton Park lines.

January 17th - Last day of services for Walsall-Rugeley, Coventry-Nuneaton and Coventry-Leamington.

February 27th - Goods workings ceased over the Wombourn line.

April 12th - Corngreaves goods branch closed.

April 12th - Bushbury shed, Wolverhampton, closed.

June 1st - Dr.Beeching succeeded as Chairman of British Railways by Stanley Raymond.

June - Leamington shed closed.

June 28th - Bromford Bridge racecourse station officially closed.

August 9th - Closure consent for the Redditch branch refused; judgment reserved in the case of Selly Oak and Bournville stations - consent to their closure refused on 25th October 1967.

October - Aston shed closed.

1966

March - Walsall power signal box becomes fully operational.

April 18th - Blackwell station closed.

May 15th - New connection between the ex-GWR and ex-LMS lines opened at Leamington Spa.

May 22nd - Stanier Pacific "City of Birmingham" arrives at Birmingham Science Museum.

1967

January - Monument Lane shed closed.

February 28th - Collision at Stechford, nine people killed.

March 3rd - Wolverhampton Oxley shed closed.

March 4th-5th - Last weekend that Birmingham Snow Hill functioned as a main line station.

March 6th - Full electric service began between Euston-Birmingham New Street-Manchester/Liverpool. Saltley shed closed to steam.

April - Stourbridge and Ryecroft sheds closed.

July 16th - Dudley Freightliner Terminal opened.

1968

March 2nd - Many local stations on the Birmingham to Derby and Leicester main lines saw their last trains on this date, including Saltley, Castle Bromwich, Coleshill, Whitacre and Kingsbury. The 'last' train ran through Snow Hill tunnel, the 17.52 to Leamington Spa. The track was removed from the tunnel the following November. Dunstall Park, west of Wolverhampton Low Level, also closed.

March 23rd - Stratford-Gloucester closed to regular passenger trains, the end of the Great Western's Birmingham-Bristol main line as a through route.

1969

January 20th - Lawley Street Freightliner teminal augmented with opening of adjacent Montague St. International Container Depot.

March 1st - Berkswell-Kenilworth direct line taken out of use.

May 2nd - Closure of North Warwickshire Line prevented by High Court Injunction.

June - Bromsgrove station "rebuilt" - one platform only, on northbound line.

July 14th - Snow Hill mural opened in St.Chad's Circus underpass.

August - Saltley power box became operational.

1970

January 3rd - Last day of Hartlebury-Bewdley and Kidderminster-Bewdley passenger service.

May 4th - Wolverhampton Low Level station became a Parcels Concentration Depot.

September 13th - Lord Mayor of Birmingham formally opens the depot for preserved steam at Tyseley, now Birmingham Railway Museum.

December 7th -Dudley-Edinburgh Freightliner service begins.

1972

January 1st - Responsibility for local rail services passes to West Midlands Passenger Transport Authority (WMPTA)

March 4th - Last day of services between Birmingham Snow Hill and Wolverhampton Low Level (and also of the link service between Snow Hill and Langley Green), the last closure of the century for a West Midlands' local passenger service.

May 1st - Birmingham New Street established as the hub of the long distance rail network.

May 5th - Oxley carriage sidings, Wolverhampton, electrified - a small section of ex-Great Western line receives the same treatment as the ex-LNWR West Coast Main Line.

Notes

The 1960s have entered railway folklore as the 'Beeching Era'. Richard Beeching, a director of ICI, was appointed Chairman of the British Transport Commission (BTC) with effect from 1st June 1961, becoming Chairman of the British Railways Board (BRB) when it replaced the BTC at the beginning of 1963. The Minister of Transport, Ernest Marples, agreed to match his ICI salary of £24,000 - colossal for the time - which compared favourably with the £10,000 of Beeching's predecessor and the £5,000 of Marples himself. Dr.Beeching was never entirely happy at the BRB; his knowledge of railways was slight. His period of office was due to end in 1966, but he returned to ICI in June 1965, at his own request.

It is said that a little knowledge is a dangerous thing, and Beeching's unfamiliarity with railways did not stop him from attempting to solve their problems in his own inimitable way. Before becoming Chairman of the BTC he was a member of the Stedeford Advisory Group, set up in 1960 to advise the Minister of Transport, who was planning an extensive road-building programme (the first part of the M1 had opened in 1959). Within this group Beeching expressed strong opposition to electrification of the West Coast Main Line, which had been a part of the 1955 Modernisation Plan. He thought that diesels would do the job better! Fortunately neither Stedeford nor even Marples agreed with him and electrification was endorsed in January 1961.

2-6-2T No.4555 was privately purchased, restored and repainted at Tyseley during 1964, ready for preservation. It hauled some private charter trains, including an SLS five coach tour on June 13th, from Snow Hill to Dudley and the Bromyard line. The loco now operates on the Dart Valley line, between Paignton and Kingswear. *(Jones family collection - courtesy of Locomotives International)*

Beeching's time in office saw wholesale closures and cutbacks of lines throughout the country. His 148-page report, "The Reshaping of British Railways" was published on Wednesday 27th March 1963. The West Midlands suburban rail network was never as extensive as those in other conurbations of similar size, notably Manchester and Glasgow. This did not spare some lines from closure leaving, for example, a town the size of Dudley without a train service. Walsall was the hub of five routes; by January 1965 they had been cut to one. Places that escaped the axe found themselves with a reduced service that was virtually useless, a gross insult to those who had fought hard to prevent closure. Thanks in part to media speculation, many more train services had the threat of closure, real or imagined, hanging over them.

Beeching's main fault was his attitude. The only cure he could offer for a "loss making" line was that it should be put down. Had he been a doctor of medicine rather than a chemist he would have wreaked havoc in the NHS! No positive alternatives were considered. The social value of a secondary line, the way it fed passengers into main line services, the methods by which its costs could be reduced or its train service improved - none of these factors entered his equation. On freight, the good doctor was proud of his Big Idea, liner trains, out of which grew the Freightliner network. All well and good, but the development of these trains, with West Midland terminals at Dudley and Birmingham Lawley Street, could not hide the haemorrhaging of general freight. Station sidings and small goods yards closed, the railways' own fleet of delivery vehicles declined. The volume of wagonload traffic fell away. Important facilities, notably Birmingham Central Goods yard, closed completely.

The withdrawal of services and the race to scrap steam were accompanied by a growth in awareness of the railways' past and its value; an increase in nostalgia for the imagined era when all trains ran to time, the birth of today's multi-million pound railway heritage industry. As stations closed they were stripped of all their fixtures and fittings, some of which were highly desirable items for enthusiasts. At first it was possible to buy them at scrap value or less. A station name sign, a totem, could be had for just ten shillings (50p); today many are worth hundreds of pounds. Locomotive nameplates were easily available to private collectors. Others went to very appropriate homes. "Hartlebury Castle" went to the entrance hall there, "Sir William A.Stanier FRS." is displayed in the lobby of Stanier House, Birmingham.

The elimination of steam was not entirely ruthless. Its end as part of the everyday railway was inevitable, but its supporters were ready to ensure that something was left for future generations to appreciate and enjoy. The Severn Valley Railway was a victim of the Beeching cuts. It reopened in stages between Bridgnorth and Kidderminster until it became, in the words of its own publicity, "Britain's premier steam railway". Since the bulk of its expansion occurred in the 1980s, its growth and progress will best be described in Volume Three. In Birmingham, the steam shed at Tyseley closed in 1967 and most of it was demolished two years later. During the interim, the former coaling stage was converted into a small shed specifically for housing preserved locos. An extension was built and doors fitted at both ends. The terms of the lease allowed locos access to the surviving turntable. As early as 6th June 1968 there was a cermony here to mark the restoration of a "Jubilee" class loco, 5593 "Kolhapur" which was once again in LMS livery. In those early days the new shed was open only to organised parties and by prior appointment, but during an Open Day on 13th September 1970 the Lord Mayor of Birmingham formally opened the steam depot. Since then, what is now the Birmingham Railway Museum has, like the Severn Valley Railway, grown in popularity, thanks to the unabating fascination with steam.

Some locomotives were obvious candidates for preservation; nobody contemplated scrapping "Mallard" or "King George V". In the same vein, civic pride meant that Stanier Pacific No.46235 "City of Birmingham" was acquired by the city after withdrawal. It was transferred to Crewe, from whence it was outshopped in British Railways green livery, before the final handover. On Sunday 22nd May 1966 "City of Birmingham" made the three mile road journey from Lawley Street to the Museum of Science and Industry in Newhall Street. Loco and tender made separate journeys. On arrival, the tender first, they were lowered onto a section of track alongside the museum and encased in weatherproof sheeting. The building was soon extended around this new prize exhibit, visible from the street through huge windows. Every hour a mechanism would be activated by museum staff and "City of Birmingham", like a caged lion, slowly travelled a distance of six feet or so, to the accompaniment of taped sound effects, reverse and come to rest. The museum was housed in Elkington's former electro-plating factory and was home to many interesting industrial items, including working examples of James Watt steam engines and a Spitfire, over half the total number of which were built at Castle Bromwich. Its displays had hardly changed since the 1950s, nothing of real consequence had happened since the arrival of "City of Birmingham". Despite this it remained popular but instead of modernising it, the city fathers decided to close it down at the end of 1997, leaving the exhibits to languish unseen for almost four years, until the opening of a new 'Discovery Centre' at Millenium Point in 2001.

Birmingham Inner Ring Road, a product of the 1950s and 60s, has six major intersections, each with a large traffic island or 'circus'. Some have pedestrian access via subways and paths across the island itself. St.Chad's Circus, between Snow Hill station and the Roman Catholic cathedral, is enlivened by a mural on the island's retaining wall. It is a mosaic, accurately illustrating the history of the station from its opening in 1852 until 1967. There are early Great Western signals, a broad gauge train, porters with luggage, etc. It was commissioned by the city's Public Works Department at a cost of £30,000 and was unveiled by the Deputy Lord Mayor on 14th July 1969. At a variable height, ranging up to sixteen feet, and with a length of 300 feet, it is probably the largest wall-mounted mosaic in the world, a remarkable if little known work of public art and a tribute to a much-loved station which, by 1969, was about to have its life-support system switched off.

Stations

All five major stations in the West Midlands experienced profound change during the 1960s. Three were completely rebuilt, two were all but closed.

The most successful rebuild was Coventry. The station it replaced had just two platforms and an earlier improvement scheme, begun in 1939, was halted by the war. This time a completely new station would replace the old, from the ballast up. The track layout was improved. Previously there were four tracks, one for each platform with up and down fast lines through the centre. The new station would have four platforms, all long enough for a 16-coach train. Connections with the Leamington line were modified so that its trains could enter and leave at Platform 1, on the down slow line, which was signalled bi-directionally. This avoided conflict with main line traffic to Birmingham, which used Platform 3. At one stage during the rebuilding neither the new nor old footbridge was available for use by parcels traffic, which was transferred from one platform to the other courtesy of a diesel shunter and a single wagon. The station opened on 1st March 1962, a few months ahead of Coventry's new cathedral. The buildings are simple - stark even - but elegant, plain and functional. After withdrawal, a name and numberplate from 46240 "City of Coventry" were mounted in a prominent position on the footbridge. The station is now a listed building.

Ad hoc arrangements during the rebuilding of Coventry station, 13th June 1961. 0-4-0 diesel hydraulic loco D2911 (with North British Loco.Co. plates clearly visible) stands at the new Platform 4. Parcels are being loaded onto the wagon for transfer to the southbound (up) side of the station, as no bridge existed between the platforms at this stage in the proceedings. Note the baby buggy! *(Michael Mensing)*

The leading locomotive - BR Standard No.75036 - is the only really new thing in this photograph. The other loco is ex-LMS Stanier Class 5 No.44837. The pair are hauling a northbound train, probably empty stock, a mixture of corridor and non-corridor vehicles, through Coventry on 5th September 1953.   *(H.F.Wheeler collection : courtesy of Roger Carpenter)*

The clean lines of Coventry station when new, with a Park Royal dmu on a train for Nuneaton (service suspended 1965-1988). The original caption read, "A typical modern railway station which may be provided at Redditch to give quick access to Birmingham"!

(courtesy of Birmingham Post & Mail)

Birmingham New Street is a different matter entirely. The 1960s station is a master stroke in the art of deception. Its developers never saw it principally as a station but as a valuable site capable of generating large amounts of revenue for them. As such the trains and their passengers - inconvenient necessities - were to be confined to a hole in the ground. This telling passage appeared in "Railway Magazine" for June 1963 - *The redevelopment proposals take full advantage of the high commercial value of the site and the fact that the platforms and track are below ground level. The upper levels will, it is anticipated, comprise a new shopping precinct, an entertainments centre, restaurants and car parking*".

Compared with the old station, the 1960s New Street could handle more trains more easily. From virtually every other standpoint it has been a disaster. The old New Street was really two stations, separated by a road, Queen's Drive, and spanned by a footbridge which formed a public right of way. War damage and neglect made rebuilding inevitable. Queen's Drive was eliminated, giving more space for the platform area. The old station had eight through platforms and six bays. Four of the bays, on the LNWR side, were joined up as a preliminary to rebuilding. This created two temporary through platforms, vital when others would be out of commission. The layout of the new station consisted of twelve through platforms, all able to accommodate one full length or two short trains, as they had mid-point signals. Seven platforms were signalled bi-directionally. All trains entering or leaving by the London end had access to all twelve platforms. At the Wolverhampton end, all trains to/from Wolverhampton had access to all twelve platforms; trains for the West Suburban line (the main line to Bristol) could enter and leave Platforms 5-12. This greatly enhanced the capacity of the station, easily able to handle the 250 (approx.) train movements per day which were then the norm. (Now that train movements have risen to more than 750, the track layout is under greater pressure than ever before.)

New Street suffers from being submerged under a 7½ acre concrete raft, supported by over 200 columns. The raft is set at a very low level above the tracks, the minimum possible to give clearance for the overhead electrification wires. This has a claustrophobic effect. The underside of the raft, above the wires, is permanently filthy, Railtrack are making (1998) brave efforts to brighten the platform areas with improved tiling and lighting, but it still holds true that you cannot make a silk purse from a sow's ear. Escalators travel up from the platforms, but none go down. The stairs are awkward for passengers with luggage, the lifts are not well signposted. The staff are aware of the shortcomings of New Street and strive hard to help people in difficulties.

The right of way formed by the old footbridge had to be retained in the new station. It was kept in the letter but not in the spirit, arranged so that it took an indirect route, past as many retail outlets as possible. Worse, it no longer gave access directly onto either Stephenson Street or Station Street. As the new station emerged from the building site and commuters became aware of this there were howls of protest. The entrances had just a short stay of execution, for rush hour traffic only. The planners were so out of touch with the needs of passengers that the main entrance was constructed facing the Inner Ring Road! The service road between the station and ring road is narrow and contorted. There is no space for a bus stop, just a few 20-minute parking spaces and an area permanently clogged with taxis.

The concourse is light and pleasant, almost attractive, a relief when emerging from platform level. It remains uninspired and ordinary, but used to have pretensions of its own. Who now remembers the restaurant, where John Menzies is situated, which

had aisles for the waitresses between the rows of tables? Each table had two lights for customers' use, green to summon a waitress, red to call the wine waiter! Above this level are the many retail outlets. Access to the city centre is via a crowded ramp which leads down to the corner of New Street and Corporation Street.

New Street station remains a fascinating place, with large numbers of people and a wide variety of train services. It is helped by the visible presence of staff, especially at platform level. Had it been built purely as a railway station its problems would be few; as it is they appear intractable.

Wolverhampton High Level was rebuilt between February 1964 and March 1967, again in conjunction with electrification. The old station had three through platforms (a side and an island) and a bay at the Birmingham end. Its alignment meant that the overall roof often acted as a wind tunnel. Like the Midland side of New Street, it was still gas lit and in urgent need of attention. In 1961 there were plans for the roof to be removed, the buildings to be retained and improved and an extra island platform to be added to the north, which would have given it five full-length platforms. The old buildings were found to be unsafe, so revised plans of 1963 provided for their complete demolition and replacement, the lengthening of the existing platforms and abandoning of the extra island platform. The station is in 1960s Concrete Ordinary style. At first there were complaints about the short platform canopies and the lack of amenities on the island platform. In swift response, British Rail lengthened the canopies by 120 feet and added a buffet, waiting room and toilets on the island platform by the end of 1967. There have been further improvements since, notably the conversion of a short north-facing goods bay into Platform 1c in 1979, used by Shrewsbury locals. With expanded train services in recent years Wolverhampton, like New Street, is suffering capacity problems. The unbuilt island platform would have been useful. Even in 1967, the name boards on the new station read simply 'Wolverhampton', an ominous snub to its neighbour.

The ex-Great Western station at Low Level had two through platforms and three bays. It had once possessed an overall roof, which became unsafe and was dismantled in 1933. The station lost almost all its traffic in March 1967. The Paddington-Birkenhead trains were axed, all main line trains to London and Shrewsbury now ran from High Level. Only a few locals to Shrewsbury and the bubble car shuttle to Snow Hill remained. The Shrewsbury locals were diverted to High Level in May 1968 with the closure of Dunstall Park station. The Snow Hill shuttle continued to use the down main plaform, leaving the rest of the station virtually unused. Low Level was soon to enjoy a new role as a Parcels Concentration Depot, with a delivery area extending to Lichfield, Walsall, Dudley and Kidderminster. Hoping that bigger really would be better, it replaced smaller depots within that area and opened for business on 6th April 1970. Parcels vans used the up platform track and part of the former through lines. Much of the space between the platforms, newly surfaced, was used by road delivery vehicles. The Snow Hill bubble car continued to use a corner of the station until 1972. Low Level is now disused, the remaining track is still intact but severed by a new road across the south end of the trackbed. On closure of the parcels depot a solitary van was left behind; it remains there yet, in fading Rail Blue, surrounded by weeds.

Birmingham Snow Hill had been rebuilt between 1906 and 1912 and it was one of the finest stations in the country. Its future had seemed secure. The 1913 power signal box at the north end of the station was replaced by a new box in September 1960. The whole station was repainted in 1958-60 and in 1961 plans were announced for a complete rebuild, with platforms at

As one comes down the other goes up. Demolition of the Midland side of New Street station in progress during the summer of 1964 as the Rotunda nears completion. The Bull Ring Centre looked drab even then. Beyond, the large illuminated 'S' (for Schweppes) was a night time landmark for several years. *(courtesy of Birmingham Post & Mail)*

A Cravens dmu lurks in the gloom of the brave new New Street, 15th September 1969. *(courtesy of Railtrack)*

A Derby lightweight dmu has arrived at Redditch from New Street. This service was improved in 1960, when steam was replaced by diesel and trains ran at hourly intervals. Regular dmus never worked south of Redditch, so the steam service to Evesham and Ashchurch remained infrequent until closure.
(Rodney Blanthorn)

The overall roof at Wolverhampton High Level, looking north, 28th September 1963. *(Roger Shenton)*

one level, car parking above and a shopping arcade on the top level. None of this was to happen.

The decision to electrify the Euston-New Street route was also seen as a chance to downgrade the alternative. Snow Hill would not be required as a main line station. In the short term it bore the brunt of the London service while electrification engineering works disrupted the Euston line. Main line services ended in March 1967. A year later all trains from Leamington and Stratford stopped short at Moor Street as Snow Hill tunnel was closed. In 1969 the former Great Western Hotel was demolished. The last train left in March 1972 and the station's rotting hulk

decayed further. The space between the main line platforms was surfaced and used as a car park (30p all day!). In 1976 a British Rail surveyor inspected the building and found that it was in danger of collapse. Demolition began on 4th October and was completed the following summer.

Other lesser stations experienced a 'total environment change', even when the trains kept running. Kidderminster had a unique mock-Tudor building on the northbound platform, which was badly affected by dry rot. It was demolished in 1968 and replaced by the sort of building which features in the drawings of the average four-year-old, a boring cube alongside the platform.

No.3101 powers through Bordesley with a northbound freight. This loco was one of five members of the 3100 Class, 1938 rebuilds of the 3150 Class, dating from 1907 and still going strong in 1953.

(P.J.Garland collection, courtesy of Roger Carpenter)

Kidderminster station approach, about 1959. Not a train in sight, but look at that splendid building, soon to be demolished, not to mention the period cars! The fence marks the boundary of the goods yard, closed in 1983 and now part of a much larger car park. The house behind the station remains today and the approach road retains its stone setts.

(Roger Carpenter collection)

The long and low Birmingham platform was cut back, the remainder being raised two feet. A promised footbridge failed to materialise. Walsall lost most of its trains in 1965 and all of its platform buildings soon after. The distinctive drum-shaped booking hall of 1923, together with the glass canopy entrance from Park Street, survived until 1978, when they were demolished despite howls of protest. Redditch became a terminus when the line south to Ashchurch was severed in 1963. The ex-Midland Railway station was bulldozed in 1972 and a new island platform provided on the north side of the road bridge. This station had temporary wooden buildings which lasted until 1993. When the track profile at the foot of the Lickey Incline was improved during the summer of 1969, the loop serving Bromsgrove's southbound platform was abolished. That platform and the station buildings were all demolished, leaving just a shortened northbound platform. As there were already two crossovers here, southbound trains stopping at Bromsgrove - just one every day - could use the wrong road for a short distance, but any delay to a northbound main line train resulted in a frustrating wait just yards from the platform. The four track main line between Birmingham and Lapworth was reduced to two. The redundant platform buildings at the affected stations were demolished in 1969. Remaining buildings were 'rationalised', none more so than at Bordesley, where a small and forbidding concrete bunker was provided.

Freight

During the 1950s rail still carried half this country's freight. The huge variety of material that this represented was reflected in the wide variety of trains themselves. I can do no better than reproduce the opening pages of the Express Freight Trains Timetable, London Midland Region, for July 1957. The facts and figures speak for themselves. Of the trains listed, driver Maurice Newman, who was a fireman at the time, recalled the 3pm departure from Birmingham Lawley Street to Glasgow College, a goods station near Glasgow Cross. The 3pm had the longest non-stop run for a freight train on British Railways, 228 miles from Lawley Street to Carlisle, via the Settle-Carlisle line. Maurice fired this train for two years, out one day, returning the next, an overnight lodging turn. In the 1950s it was semi-fitted, in other words up to two-thirds of its wagons were fitted with brakes, and top speed was 45mph. Later, when fully fitted, it was increased to 60mph. The load was limited to 45 vans and wagons. This was a very popular train with freight customers because it was reliable and ran to time. Consequently there was a full load - a digger - virtually every day. The train's consist frequently included tyres from Dunlop, Cadbury's chocolate and seasonable fruit from the Vale of Evesham. Perishables always had priority. Glasgow customers could collect them from 7am, whereas other goods were only available after 12 noon. Vans and wagons were detached at Carlisle, where others would be attached, a short 40 minute breather for the train crew in a total journey time of 8 hours 45 minutes.

The loco was a Stanier Black Five or any other powerful engine that was available and in good condition. In later years the Standard Class 9Fs, nicknamed 'spaceships', were more than up to the task and the load increased from 45 to 50.

If Maurice was unfortunate enough to have a certain driver, with a reputation for thrashing the engine, it would consume 10 tons of coal on the journey, which is more than a ton per hour. *"In reality though, this meant that when the tender was full you were shovelling back some coal that spilled down from the top, so you probably shovelled close on 15 tons altogether."* Three times going north and twice coming south, Maurice emptied the tender. With another driver, who had a more gentle approach, only 6 tons would be used. On the return journey the driver would be warned by the Carlisle yardmaster if high winds were expected on the exposed tops of the route to Settle, he would ask if it was a good engine and, if there was a wind of Force 6 or more, the driver had the option of reducing the length of the train. Maurice's very last trip on this train was a windy one, the regulator was open wide, the loco was at full stretch, yet they were down to a slow walking pace at Ais Gill summit. When the daily car-carrying trains from King's Norton to Bathgate (near Edinburgh) first started using this route the cars were transported on flat wagons and just 'scotched' down. *"It was possible to go onto Blea Moor viaduct with ten cars and come off with just four or five."* The tractors and farm machinery carried on the return journey sometimes had a similar experience, so it was not long before the vehicles were secured more substantially.

FACTS ABOUT FREIGHT SERVICES

Some 17,600 freight trains are run daily by British Railways.

Each weekday 591 express freight trains—300 more than before the war—are now operated and this number will be increased greatly in the near future.

During 1956 over 277 million tons of revenue-earning freight were conveyed—nearly a million tons every working day of the year.

Over 70 per cent of the total deep-mined coal needing transport is carried by British Railways.

The present total stock of wagons in use exceeds a million, 187,000 of which are now fitted with continuous brakes for high-speed working. In 1956, 61,474 new vehicles were built; 69,000 are scheduled for completion this year.

The number of containers in use has risen from 15,511 in 1938 to 35,833 in 1956. A further big expansion is in progress.

The fleet of motor vehicles used for collection and delivery services now totals 15,846 units, the numbers of horsedrawn vehicles having decreased from 22,576 in 1948 to 1,224 in 1956.

PRINCIPAL EXPRESS FREIGHT TRAIN SERVICES

NOTES

D	Daily	FX	Fridays Excepted
FSX	Fridays and Saturdays	MX	Mondays Excepted
	Excepted	SX	Saturdays Excepted

N.B.—In the main alternative week-end services exist where trains are shown as not running on Fridays or Saturdays.

From BIRMINGHAM, ASTON

10.15 pm	SX	Manchester, London Road	—	8.00 am

From BIRMINGHAM, CURZON STREET

10.10 pm	SX	Liverpool, Edge Hill		—	8.00 am
10.20 pm	SX	London, Broad Street		—	8.00 am
		„ Camden		—	8.00 am

From BIRMINGHAM, LAWLEY STREET

Departs	Days of Week	Destination	Normally available for delivery	
			Market traffic	Ordinary traffic
3.00 pm	SX	Glasgow, College	7.00 am	12 noon
3.30 pm	D	Leeds, Hunslet Lane	6.30 am	9.00 am
8.15 pm	D	Peterborough	—	8.00 am
9.55 pm	D	Leeds, Hunslet Lane	6.30 am	9.00 am
8.00 pm	D	London, St. Pancras	—	8.00 am
10.45 pm	D	Sheffield, Queen's Road	6.00 am	7.30 am
8.50 pm	D	York	6.00 am	9.30 am

From WALSALL

8.45 pm	SX	Liverpool, Edge Hill	—	8.00 am
8.45 pm	SX	London, Camden	—	8.00 am
8.45 pm	SX	Manchester, London Road	—	8.00 am

From WOLVERHAMPTON

9.15 pm	SX	Liverpool, Edge Hill	—	8.00 am
8.33 pm	SX	London, Camden	—	8.00 am
9.15 pm	SX	Manchester, London Road	—	8.00 am

Extracts from the London Midland Region timetable of 'Principal Express Freight Train Services and Facilities' for July 1957.

(Michael Denholm)

Rebuilt 'Patriot' 4-6-0 No.45532 "Illustrious" with a Washwood Heath-Manchester fitted freight at Water Orton, 1962.

(Maurice Newman)

General freight in the year of the Modernisation Plan, 1955. 0-6-0 No.44135 heads south past the site of the present Longbridge station.

(Roger Carpenter collection, courtesy Don Powell)

Less than a year separates the 'before' and 'after' photographs of Bescot yard, taken on 15th October 1964 and 9th September 1965. The point of reference common to both is the Wellman Smith Owen mechanical coaling plant. The newly installed Dowty retarders occupy the foreground in the 1965 picture. Wagons shunted over the down yard hump (behind the camera) could be more effectively controlled by the retarders, minimising the risk of damage or collision. They were worked on a piston system controlled by the signalman, whereby the air would push up the horseshoe-shaped retarders, which can be seen in groups alongside each rail. In this way they applied pressure on wheels passing over them. They were very effective, but installed at a time when wagonload traffic was in decline and fewer trains needed sorting, so they never fulfilled their potential. They lay disused for many years and were removed in the early 1990s.

Bescot Yard on 15th October 1964 ....

.... and on 9th September 1965

(both - courtesy of Railtrack)

Dudley Freightliner terminal, where Dudley station once stood, opened on 16th July 1967 and the accompanying photograph shows it as new. Passenger services to Dudley had ceased in 1964 and the Dudley-Wolverhampton line, reduced to a single track diversion round the terminal site, closed in 1968, although the length seen here was retained as a headshunt. The Stourbridge-Dudley-Walsall line snakes across the foreground past the 1960's signalbox. Trains to/from the Walsall direction had to reverse out of/into the terminal. Dudley had its own trains to Glasgow and Nottingham and the Newcastle-Cardiff Freightliner also called there. Ray Churchill remembered the hazards of the Nottingham train, *"a nice little day turn"*, because it carried 8' 6" high containers, only just within the loading gauge. On the freight line south of Derby, between Stenson Junction and Trent, there were several bridges which had to be passed at 10mph. Some had brickwork which bore the scars of speeding Freightliners. Dudley closed when traffic was transferred to the ever expanding Lawley Street.

The 'before' shot of Lawley Street was taken on 10th July 1967, just before work began on construction of new Freightliner facilities. There were small containers here, of the type mentioned in the 1957 freight timetable, a travelling Ransome-Simms gantry crane and some ex-Midland Railway signals. All rather primitive when compared to the new terminal, as seen on 6th November 1969. Lawley Street had services to Harwich, Liverpool, Southampton, Hull, Manchester and Felixstowe and was expecting to handle up to 10,000 containers annually. The containers sitting directly on the track, left foreground, are either empty, or they do not form part of any of the trains being made up in the yard. These two tracks were later realigned and converted for normal use. To the right is the Customs Shed, part of the New Shed opened in 1943, with a rake of Continental vans alongside it.

Dudley Freightliner Terminal in pristine condition, 16th August 1967.

(courtesy of Railtrack)

Lawley Street goods yard, Birmingham, seen on 10th July 1967. *(courtesy of Railtrack)*

Lawley Street Freightliner Terminal, 6th November 1969. *(courtesy of Railtrack*

As the Freightliners were making their mark, traditional goods traffic was in decline. The ex-Midland Railway Central Goods station, near the heart of Birmingham city centre, closed at the end of 1966. The most historic closure victim was Curzon Street, demolished in 1966. This had been the London & Birmingham Railway terminus, opening in 1838. It closed to passengers when New Street opened in 1854. During its 111 year life as a goods station it retained much of its dignity and many original features. The adjacent Grand Junction station at Curzon Street (1839), which had also been used for goods after 1854, was demolished in 1971. The Grand Junction's first Wolverhampton station (1837) at Wednesfield Heath, closed to passengers in 1873 but remained open for general goods until October 1965.

Smaller yards and station sidings closed in large numbers. Goods facilities were withdrawn and small businesses were discouraged from using rail. For example, the North Warwickshire Line lost its last remaining freight trains in 1968. At the end these had consisted of a Bordesley-Stratford round trip on Mondays and Thursdays and a Bordesley-Hall Green round trip on Tuesdays and Fridays. Normal traction was a Type 4 diesel. The last train ran on Friday 3rd May and the goods depots at Hall Green, Shirley and Stratford closed. In September that year, general freight facilities were withdrawn from Halesowen (closed to passengers in 1927), Soho (closed to passengers in 1949), Handsworth & Smethwick, Tyseley and Wednesbury Central.

Some former passenger lines remained open for goods but the 1960s took a heavy toll. The Wombourn line closed to passengers in 1932. It remained open for freight and proved its worth as a useful alternative route during World War Two. As goods traffic declined it was surplus to requirements, closing after the passage of the last train on 27th February 1965. The Halesowen line remained in use for goods until January 1964. The rickety viaduct over Dowery Dell was dismantled during the spring of 1965.

The Harborne line closed to passengers in 1934, but freight continued, chiefly house coal for Harborne and Hagley Road stations, timber for the Chad Valley toy factory and traffic to and from Mitchells & Butlers brewery at Cape Hill, which had its own spur off the branch. The sidings at Harborne were also used to store coaches, especially at busy periods when Monument Lane sidings were full. On one notable occasion, an elderly ex-Midland 0-6-0, No.58185, hauled a 10 coach corridor train unassisted up the 1:66 Woodbourne Bank from Harborne towards Hagley Road. The stock had been used by Covent Garden Opera on a visit to Birmingham and was now being reclaimed, 30th April 1952, for use as a football excursion. The first passenger train to Harborne since 1934 was a push-pull special on 3rd June 1950, organised by the Stephenson Locomotive Society. Another SLS special followed on 30th May 1959. Birmingham University Railway & Inland Waterway Society organised a 60 mile railtour (fare 16 shillings - 80p) on 17th March 1962, the only time a diesel multiple unit ventured onto the branch. The Harborne line would have been closed in the Beeching era in any event, but the most important nail in its coffin was Mitchells & Butlers' decision to switch from rail to road transport. The line was to close and once again the treasurer of the SLS swung into action. This was the respected railway photographer from Handsworth, W.A.Camwell, known as 'Cam'. He organised the very last passenger train over both the Harborne and Halesowen lines, which ran on Saturday 2nd November 1963. All 320 seats were sold about ten days earlier. The train was topped and tailed by two of Bescot's ex-LMS 2-6-0s, 46429 and 46522. It was seen off from New Street by the bowler hatted stationmaster, along with several hundred enthusiasts. On arrival at Harborne it stopped short of the platform, with many passengers jumping down and swarming onto the tracks, mingling with local people

Photo: *W. A. Camwell*

Rotton Park Road station, Harborne branch, on 22nd November, 1934, showing L.M.S.R. 0-6-2T 6924 (L.N.W.R. "Radial" class tank) on the 12-50 p.m. Birmingham New St.—Harborne.

Notes for the special which ran on 2nd November 1963, suitably lined in black.   *(Don Powell collection)*

for one last look, one last photo opportunity. The special departed and, apart from the wagon recovery and demolition trains, the line had passed from reality into memory.

In concluding this section it must be remembered that some of British Railways' biggest freight customers had internal railway systems of their own, complete with company locomotives. Even into the 1960s - but scarcely beyond - industrial locomotives were still hard at work all over the West Midlands, and the photographs here are just a small selection from a large number.

Webb tank No.46757 poses for the camera at a sunny Monument Lane with the SLS special en route to Harborne, 3rd June 1950.
(John Edgington)

One last photo opportunity. 46429 tops the train, 46522 tails it - Harborne, 2nd November 1963.
(John Edgington)

Coppice Colliery line, Cannock Chase with loco No.2 (built by Kitson in 1921), 19th October 1957. *(Roger Shenton)*

A Birmingham Tame & Rea District Drainage Board loco (built 1915), at Minworth, 4th March 1961. *(John Edgington)*

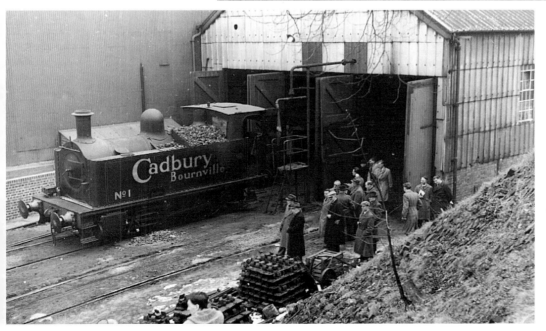

Cadbury's loco No.1 on shed, during an organised visit to Bournville, March 1955. The loco water supply pipe comes from a tank within the shed. Older men still wore hats or caps. The overcoat is challenged here by the early appearance of a duffle coat. *(Roger Carpenter collection, courtesy Don Powell)*

"Vulcan" at the Austin Works, Longbridge, 5th May 1962. The structure at the rear is an overheard conveyor to carry car components from one side of the works to the other. "Vulcan" was one of a pair, the other being "Victor", built at Bagnalls of Stafford on 1950. They had American tri-tone whistles, enclosed bearings and were very strong. Maintenance was carried out at Tyseley. Both locos are preserved. *(John Edgington)*

No.3, built in 1920, seen at Fort Dunlop about 1960. *(John Edgington)*

Who says industrial railways can't look attractive ? 0-6-0 saddle tank "Jubilee", hard at work on the Pensnett Railway, 1st May 1958.
(Roger Shenton)

0-6-0 tank engine No.13, built by Robert Stephenson & Hawthorns and owned by the Central Electricity Authority, hauls a rake of loaded coal wagons into Hams Hall Power Station, Sunday 26th November 1967.
(Michael Mensing)

Stanier 4-6-0 "Jubilee" Class No.45647 "Sturdee" leaves Birmingham New Street with the up "Midlander", September 1956. Perhaps the claret and blue roofboards were the work of an Aston Villa supporter?   *(Colour -Rail/BRM1205)*

All the "Kings" were temporarily withdrawn for several weeks, whilst a fault discovered on the front bogies was modified. Locos were loaned from the London Midland Region and here Pacific No.46237 "City of Bristol" arrives at Birmingham Snow Hill with a train of assorted Great Western stock, May 1955.   *(Colour-Rail/BRW722)*

"Castle" No.7014 "Caerhays Castle" with a northbound express from the West of England, near The Lakes Halt, North Warwickshire Line, summer of 1959.

(Colour -Rail/BRW 768)

6026 "King John" leaves Snow Hill tunnel with the up "Cambrian Coast Express" and its rake of chocolate and cream Mark I stock. The crane is putting the finishing touches to Rackham's department store, 1959.

(Colour-Rail/BRW 739)

A new Derby-built Class 116 dmu at Snow Hill's Platform 8 1957. *(Colour -Rail/DE 856)*

Class 101 Metro-Cammell dmu at Four Oaks, brand new, with a Derby Lightweight unit alongside. April 1959. *(Colour-Rail/DE1742)*

A Gloucester Carriage & Wagon built Class 122 bubble car (W55000 series) forms the 16.47 service from Langley Green to Birmingham Snow Hill on 5th August 1967. The train is crossing the bridge over Telford's canal, where the Jewellery Line platforms of Galton Bridge station were to open in 1995.

(Michael Mensing)

The "Birmingham Pullman" waits at Snow Hill's Platform 5 to return to Paddington with the 13.00 service, having arrived there with the 10.10 ex-Paddington. This was the train's normal departure platform.

(Robert Darlaston)

Ex-LMS 'Jubilee' No.45662 Kempenfelt with a southbound train through Selly Oak, 9th April 1959. *(Roger Shenton)*

An evocative shot of two steam expresses, seen from the east end of the platforms at Castle Bromwich, Saturday 5th September 1959. To the left, a British Railways Standard (Class 5) 4-6-0, No.73028, heads what is probably a return holiday train from the West of England or Bournemouth. The label on the carriage window reads 'Sheffield'. Ex-LMS 'Jubilee' 4-6-0 No.45690 "Leander" passes Castle Bromwich Junction signal box and approaches the camera with the 12.52pm York-Bristol. *(Michael Mensing)*

BR Standard Class 5MT No.73015 climbs the Lickey with a cross country express, late summer 1956. Blood and custard gives way to maroon.
(Colour -Rail/BRM518)

Ex-LMS 4F (Fowler, 1924) 0-6-0 No.44123 (with tall chimney) enters Bromsgrove with the 5.46pm New Street-Gloucester stopping train, August 1956.
(Colour-Rail/BRW367)

A re-engined 1470hp Brush diesel-electric, D5532, passes the site of Monument Lane shed with an empty stock working towards New Street, 31st August 1968. In the background, the temporary devastation caused by slum clearance is almost total. *(Michael Mensing)*

A Class 310 emu, looking smart in Rail Blue, passes the site of Monument Lane shed with the 14.40 local service from New Street to Wolverhampton, 31st August 1968. The full-end yellow warning panel had arrived, but headcodes and first class accommodation had not yet departed. The top of the art gallery clock tower can be seen. *(Michael Mensing)*

Beginnings ....

The most important improvement to the railways of the West Midlands in the 1960s was the electrification of the West Coast Main Line. This included the long loop between Rugby and Stafford, via Coventry, Birmingham and Wolverhampton. It also encompassed the line to Walsall, Bescot yard, the Grand Junction freight line (Birmingham-Wolverhampton and Bushbury Junction via Bescot), Darlaston Junction-Pleck Junction, the Soho Loop, Stechford-Aston and Windsor St. Goods (closed 1980). Plans to electrify to Lichfield via Four Oaks and from Walsall to Rugeley were abandoned after land for a new emu depot had been prepared at Ryecroft.

Electrification itself was only part of the project. Much of the track was relaid with continuous welded rail for smooth fast running. Bridges were raised and the trackbed lowered to permit clearance of the overhead wires. The main stations, as has been seen, were competely rebuilt. Many smaller stations were given a facelift. Some had their platform canopies cut back, a necessary disfigurement for the sake of clearance. The minor station at Hampton-in-Arden received particular attention. Its attractive chalet booking hall at street level was replaced and full length platforms provided. Inter City trains were to call here at peak times, as the station was within easy driving distance of Solihull, whose service to London was to be downgraded. Hampton-in-Arden fulfilled this role until after Birmingham International opened in 1976.

Certain bottlenecks were eased, notably at Rugby, where the flyover carrying trains from Birmingham clear of the Trent Valley lines was opened in September 1962. Electric trains reached Rugby from Euston in November 1964. When the wires reached Coventry some Bescot drivers were sent to Euston to learn the art of electric loco driving on a simulator. Accompanied by an instructor, they were then allowed to drive a main line express, something of a culture shock after diesel-hauled freight trains.

All signalling on the West Midlands electrified lines was converted to colour light, controlled from the power boxes at New Street, Coventry, Wolverhampton and Walsall. Together they controlled 85 route miles (192 track miles) and replaced 64 manual boxes. New Street was the last to be commissioned, on 3rd July 1966. It controlled 36 route miles (80 track miles) out to Berkswell, Hamstead, Church Road Junction (Five Ways), Tipton and Exchange Sidings (Derby line). The box is sited at the west end of the station, where the turntable once was. The exterior is clad in concrete, ridged horizontally, imposing but permanently grubby. If cleaned properly it would look good. To general amazement it achieved listed status in 1996. This is most definitely not Great Western territory, but the box is on the corner of Navigation Street and Brunel Street.

Less than a week before the full electric service began there was a collision at Stechford, on Tuesday 28th February 1967. The 13.15 semi-fast from Manchester Piccadilly to Euston, a Class 304 four-car electric multiple unit, left New Street on time at 15.34 for its non-stop run to Coventry. Approaching Stechford station at about 60mph it was struck on the side by a diesel shunter, working the yard but fouling the main line. The whole train was derailed, the first two cars thrown across the up line. Track was damaged and the overhead wires brought down. The impact was such that nine people were killed and eleven badly injured. The driver of another train had a view that was far too close for comfort. William West was in the cab of his Class 304 emu, working a Coventry-New Street stopping train, which was standing at Stechford station. He was quoted in the "Evening Mail" as saying, *The electric train shot over onto its side and tore along the track towards me at a terrific speed. It stopped about 60 yards from my cab. There was complete silence afterwards. I jumped straight out of my cab and ran into the station .... to call for ambulances and the fire brigade. It was a terrible mess and I could see that help was badly needed."*

This tragedy did not delay the full electric service, which began on Monday 6th March 1967. There were hourly stopping trains between Wolverhampton, Birmingham and Coventry and an hourly semi-fast service between New St. and Euston via Northampton, all worked by emus. The Euston semi-fasts were normally worked by Class 310s, which were then brand new, built at Derby 1965-7. The Inter-city trains were hauled by Class 81 locos in Electric Blue livery. Production Mark II coaches had been built since early 1965 and these were in evidence on many trains. There was an hourly Inter-city service between Euston, New Street and Wolverhampton, with trains continuing to Manchester and Liverpool alternately. Southbound morning peak trains called at Hampton-in-Arden to pick up and Watford Junction to set down, the reverse happening in the evening. Shrewsbury had a solitary morning through train to Euston with an evening return. The main business train from New Street was the 07.50 which, together with the 17.50 return from Euston was marketed as "The Executive" and seen as a replacement for the "Birmingham Pullman". It was *specially equipped to provide a high proportion of dining seats which will be reservable in advance and for which a supplement will be charged."* (Railway Magazine, March 1967). Most trains took an unprecedented 1 hour 35 minutes between New Street and Euston, including the Coventry stop.

The service's daily timespan was short by present standards. The first Inter-city for Euston left New St. at 07.25 (now 05.24), the last left at 20.15 (now 23.09). In the down direction, times were 08.15 (06.40) and 22.40 (23.45). The new service was a success, with the number of passengers rising steadily every year. The 1967 hourly pattern was supplemented by three morning up trains and two down in the evening. The morning and evening peaks became half-hourly in both directions in May 1969. Growth continued, passenger numbers increasing by 14% during 1970. To cope with rising demand and anxious to keep a competitive edge, the London Midland Region increased the off-peak frequency between New Street and Euston to half-hourly at the start of the new time-table on 1st May 1972.

"The LMR is to be congratulated on its bold bid to increase its already high share of the passenger business between the West Midlands and London and for being the first organisation in the world to provide an inter-city service of such frequency over comparable distances" (Brian Perren, "Modern Railways" March 1972).

One casualty was "The Executive", a non-standard train with two kitchens, under-employed for most of the day. The May 1972 timetable changes also recast the cross country services through New Street, establishing the station as the hub of British Rail's long distance passenger network. The Euston-Birmingham-Manchester or Liverpool trains had loaded very well - south of Birmingham. They no longer ventured north of Wolverhampton. Instead, trains from Manchester/Liverpool continued through New Street to destinations in the south west, such as Bristol, Cardiff or Plymouth. They were timed to give good connections at New Street with services to/from the East Midlands, Sheffield and the North East. Few people actually enjoy changing trains, so the pain was eased almost to vanishing point at New Street by ensuring that connecting trains shared the same island platform.

The 1972 timetable began after a programme of track improvements had been completed, especially on the Bristol line, where the kink at the foot of the Lickey had been ironed out. Continuous welded rail between Barnt Green and Yate helped

The new electric railway? Class 304 emu, 304 021 arrives at Oldbury with the 13.44 Stafford-New St., 22nd February 1975

(Michael Mensing)

Electric loco No.86229 emerges from New St. tunnel with the 16.29 Wolverhampton -Euston, 23rd August 1975. The old Moor St. station is visible above.

(Michael Mensing)

A three-car Metro-Cammell built dmu in original livery, including a third line parallel with the base of the window lights, arrives at Hampton-in-Arden with the 2.50pm from Birmingham New Street to Coventry and Leamington Spa (Avenue), Sunday 15th June 1958. Metro Cammell built large numbers of these cars (Class 101 and 102) between 1956 and 1960.

(Michael Mensing)

The 13.05 Euston-New Street semi-fast arrives at Hampton-in-Arden, 11th May 1974. The station was served by these semi-fasts and by peak hour InterCity trains. It was downgraded after Birmingham International opened, the further part of each platform is now closed and only local trains call there. The leading unit is 310 087; members of the 310 Class were built at Derby, 1965-67. *(Michael Mensing)*

raise the line speed to 90 mph and, for the first time, start-to-stop journeys at 60mph between New Street and Temple Meads were possible. These improvements were also spurred on by the opening of the M5 south of its junction with the M50 and the likelihood of coach competition. A 1971 application by Associated Motorways to run four coaches a day between Birmingham and Bristol, to which BR had objected, was rejected by the West Midlands Traffic Commissioners on the grounds that it was a main inter-city rail route with insufficient room for two public transport services (sic).

There were an unprecedented 13 trains linking the North East with the South West. The Leeds-Penzance "Cornishman" was accelerated by 34 minutes, the Leeds-Paignton "Devonian" by 28 minutes. The whole cross country service pattern through New Street was extremely complex, involving all five BR regions in two years of careful planning, but the idea - like most good ideas - was simple, straightforward and successful. A brief look at the current timetable (Table 51) will confirm that it still works well.

.... & Endings

A glance at the diary section which began this chapter will show how swiftly the end came for steam as shed after shed closed. Bescot remained open, but closed to steam in 1966, Tyseley followed suit early in 1967. Stanley Raymond, who succeeded Dr.Beeching in 1965, was still an ordinary member of the BRB in 1964 when he spoke about the modernisation of British Railways involving a huge scrap drive. Five hundred locomotives, 4,000 coaches, 130,000 wagons, a quarter of a million tons of rail and four ships were sold for scrap in 1963, generating an income of £20 million. Five hundred locos averaged fewer than 10 per week; during 1964 they were cut up at a rate of 75 a week, rising to close on a hundred by the end of the year. At the beginning of 1963 there were 8,767 active steam locos on British Railways, by the end of 1965 this had shrunk to 2,987. By the end of 1966

normal steam working had vanished from the West Midlands. Michael Mensing, a well known railway photographer who lived in the area at the time, shot his last picture of an ex-Great Western steam loco in normal service at Snow Hill, on 5th May 1966.

The Beeching Report identified 2,363 stations and about five thousand route miles for closure. Freight stations and depots were to be cut from about 900 to just one hundred. Likely job losses up to 1970 were estimated at 150,000. At a press conference on 27th March 1963 the doctor said, *"If this is going to be done, it is well it is done quickly"*. That same evening, at another press conference, the so-called Minister of Transport, Ernest Marples, commented, *"The quicker it is done the better"*.

West Midland lines up for closure to passengers were Walsall-Rugeley, Wolverhampton-Walsall-Lichfield-(Burton), the Sutton Park line, Walsall-Dudley, Dudley-Old Hill, Nuneaton-Coventry-Leamington. Birmingham-Redditch was listed as one of the "services to be modified". No mention was made of the North Warwickshire Line or the Snow Hill-Wolverhampton Low Level local trains.

All the above lines earmarked for closure had gone by January 1965. How aware of the needs of rail users was Ernest Marples? At the height of closures nationwide, lines were disposed of in batches, like aristocrats to the guillotine during the French Revolution. In consenting to closure for Wolverhampton-Burton, Walsall-Rugeley, Nuneaton-Coventry-Leamington and the Sutton Park line, "Railway Magazine" observed that, *"in each of these four cases the Minister has asked the Board to inform him in advance if they ever intend to remove the track"* (so that's alright then). The Sutton Park and Dudley-Old Hill lines were particularly easy targets, a turkey shoot, as the meagre train service had not been improved for decades. The disintegrating shacks which passed for stations between Old Hill and Dudley had been rebuilt as recently as 1957, but it was naive to expect that this alone would attract even a single extra passenger.

Class 47 No.D1595 stands at Platform 7 with the 2.45pm Birkenhead Woodside - Paddington, while ex-GW 0-6-0 Pannier tank No.9774 stands on the through road with a short freight train, 5th May 1966.
(Michael Mensing)

The end of steam meant an end to scenes such as these ....
Cleaning out the smokebox of "Jubilee" 4-6-0 No.45741 "Leinster" at Bescot, 1961 *(A.E.Wort)*

.... and track maintenance the traditional way, alongside Bescot No.2 box, Super D in attendance but not a high visibility vest or tamping machine anywhere in sight, August 1953. *(Ken Wort)*

The sordid reality of travel on the Bumble Hole line.

0-6-0pannier tank No.6422 propels the 6.04pm Old Hill-Dudley into what's left of Windmill End, 20th August 1957.   *(John Edgington)*

W14W at Baptist End Halt with the 6.04pm Dudley-Old Hill, 28th May 1956.   *(John Edgington)*

Passengers no more

The 10.50 Wolverhampton-Walsall, a two-coach push-pull train, is propelled out of Pleck by ex-LMS 2-6-2T No.41225. This was the only loco of its class shedded at Bushbury and it was always immaculate. The station closed with effect from 17th November 1958, the day the service was dieselised and extended to Brownhills, Lichfield and Burton. These trains also ceased in January 1965, but a Walsall-Wolverhampton service was restored in May 1998.

(Roger Shenton)

Token exchange at Kenilworth Junction as a southbound parcels train leaves the single line section from Coventry. The train is passing under the stone half of the bridge, dating from the opening of the Coventry-Leamington line, as a branch of the London & Birmingham Railway, in 1844. The brick portion of the bridge dates from the opening of the Berkswell line in 1884.

(Alan Searle)

2-6-0 No.46443 passes King's Norton with a southbound train for the Redditch line, about 1960.　　　　(*Peter Shoesmith*)

So far from being modified, the Birmingham-Redditch service, which had been dieselised and run at hourly intervals since 1960, had a notice of closure published on 12th August 1964, ostensibly because it was "running at a loss" of £45,940 in 1963. As with every other such line, this negative phrase took no account of the cost of replacement buses, or the wider social benefits that would follow if the service were improved. Within a week, six local businessmen formed the Redditch Passenger Action Committee, a high profile body which proved very active. The local press, chamber of trade, trades council and other institutions in the town all recognised the folly of closing the railway just as Redditch was being developed as a government designated New Town. The turkeys were fighting back.

A general election in 1964 brought a Labour government into office for the first time since 1951. The Labour party of the day claimed to be pro-rail, but more closures took place during 1965 than in any other year. Yet, on 9th September that year the

Minister of Transport, Tom Fraser, refused closure for the Redditch line on the grounds that it would cause too much hardship. However, he did sanction economies, so the service was reduced to just three trains to Birmingham in the morning peak and three returns in the evening. At one stroke it had been spared but rendered virtually useless. The three main line stations at Blackwell, Bromsgrove and Stoke Works were also considered for closure at the same time. Only Bromsgrove was saved, its service reduced to a single daily train in each direction. Two stations used by Redditch trains were Selly Oak and Bournville. Tom Fraser reserved his position on them, but when the BRB again proposed their closure one of his successors, Barbara Castle, refused consent in October 1967. The peak hour commuters at both Redditch and Bromsgrove acted as a life support system for their railway during this period of virtual closure, until the services were improved in stages during the 1980s.

Rural tranquility on the North Warwickshire Line, as 2-6-2 tank No.5104 enters Grimes Hill (now Wythall) with the 4.30pm from Moor Street to Henley-in-Arden, 28th May 1957. *(John Edgington)*

The attempt to close the North Warwickshire Line (all stations between Spring Road and Wootton Wawen inclusive) bears a striking similarity to a famous sketch by television comedians Morecambe and Wise, often repeated since it was first screened in the 1970s. Eric Morecambe was seated at the piano, playing a mangled version of the Grieg Piano Concerto, much to the frustration of their guest André Previn, who cried, "He's playing all the wrong notes!". At this Eric grabbed him warmly by the lapels, fixed him with a mock-menacing stare and said through gritted teeth, "I'm playing all the *right* notes, but not necessarily in the right order."

The NWL closure notice was published in May 1966. In September that year the NWL lost its status as part of a main line when the remaining services between Birmingham Snow Hill and Bristol via Stratford were diverted to the New Street route via the Lickey Incline. Between Stratford and Gloucester the only remaining passenger 'service' (and here the word is used in its most elastic sense) was a twice daily 'bubble car' dmu, running non-stop, as all the intervening stations had been closed (1960), even Cheltenham Malvern Road (1966). It came as no surprise when the bubble cars were withdrawn in March 1968.

There were over 1,300 objections to the closure of the NWL and the Minister of Transport, Richard Marsh, was advised that severe hardship would result if the line were to be closed. He ignored this advice and in May 1968 consented to closure, on condition that additional bus services were authorised <u>and available immediately after closure.</u> Midland Red applied for a licence to run them; five local authorities objected, saying the bus services would be inadequate. The objections were overruled and the licence granted. The local authorities appealed and a date was fixed for the appeal to be heard, 3rd June 1969. British Rail had meanwhile played a crucial right note in the wrong order, announcing that the last trains would run on Saturday 3rd May, a month before the buses could run. The local authorities applied for a High Court injunction restraining BR from closing the line. The application was heard on 28th April and rejected, but the judge did grant them leave to appeal against his decision. This appeal was heard on Friday 2nd May and this time an injunction was granted, so the trains kept running.

Unlike the Redditch commuters, users of the North Warwickshire Line emerged from this cliffhanger of a mauling with their train service intact. In 1971 the newly formed West Midlands Passenger Transport Authority initially refused financial support for the line, but had a change of heart by the end of the year. Their support continued in subsequent years and the train service gradually improved. BR applied to have the injunction lifted in 1984, but their motives were not entirely honourable .....

Birmingham Snow Hill-Wolverhampton Low Level was the 'closure that dare not speak its name' in the Beeching Report. However, with the ending of main line trains on this route once New Street was electrified, and a reduced main line service to Paddington from New Street, the Snow Hill local trains would be extremely vulnerable. The "Railway Magazine" (November 1966) outlined the likely scenario:-

"If closure of the North Warwickshire Line goes through only two of the once-extensive GWR suburban services into Birmingham will survive - those from Leamington and Kidderminster. Retention of Moor Street seems unlikely in these circumstances as these trains will be able to run into New Street over curves at Bordesley, Camp Hill and Smethwick; all these connections have been or are being relaid and improved before the introduction of regular passenger services."

This did not foresee the future expansion of rail services and the need to retain Moor Street and Snow Hill. The Bordesley and Camp Hill junctions referred to the routeing of the New St.-Paddington trains, via St.Andrews, Bordesley and Small Heath South junctions. This route was also taken by trains to Reading and the south coast before they were diverted to serve Birmingham International and Coventry in 1976. At Wolverhampton, most trains to Shrewsbury and beyond were routed from High Level after 1967, via a relaid connection between Wolverhampton North and Stafford Road junctions, a short stretch of line which had last seen regular passenger trains in 1859!

The end of Snow Hill and Low Level as main line stations, and the end of Snow Hill-Chester-Birkenhead as a main line, was marked on the weekend of 4th-5th March 1967 by the running of steam hauled specials, organised by Ian Allan Ltd.(4th) and the Stephenson Locomotive Society (5th). On the Saturday morning over two thousand people crowded onto the platforms at Snow Hill, in an atmosphere part party and part funeral. The first of two specials was named "The Zulu", arriving from Paddington for Chester with 11 coaches and 500 people on board. It was hauled by 7029 "Clun Castle", immaculately painted by Tyseley in Great Western livery, even though this was one of the last Castles to be built, in the British Railways era, in 1950. During the station stop even the driver and fireman posed for each other and other railwaymen in the cab and at rail level, taking pictures from all sorts of angles. "The Zulu" left and the second special arrived, hauled by 4079 "Pendennis Castle", built in 1924. "Clun Castle" returned with another special the following day. Both locomotives are preserved.

A Walsall-Stourport excursion train uses the link between Galton Junction and Smethwick Junction, 29th August 1966. Only freight and excursion trains used this line between the end of 1916 and the restoration of a regular Stourbridge line service from New Street in 1967. The line was disused from the late 1950s and was reopened on 1st June 1966. The new Galton Bridge station would be just out of camera range, to the left.

(Robert Darlaston)

Clear spring sunlight and steam combine to create this pleasing composition on the Camp Hill line, near St.Andrew's football ground, 19th April 1963. The loco is ex-LMS 'Crab' 2-6-0 No.42900 (banked by 43910) and the signal beyond the bridge shows that it will branch left at Bordesley Junction onto the short but useful link with the Snow Hill-Paddington line. New Street-Paddington trains followed the same route after the demise of Snow Hill as a main line station in 1967.

(Michael Mensing)

Away from the crowds at Snow Hill the photographer, almost alone, captures "The Zulu" as it passes to the side of Birmingham Moor Street, 4th March 1967.

(Roger Shenton)

A scene to chill the heart of any member of the Health and Safety Executive! Enthusiastic crowds on Snow Hill's Platform 8, awaiting the arrival of "The Zulu", 4th March 1967.

(Author's collection, from a photograph which first appeared in the 'Evening Mail')

REQUIEM

6020 "King Henry IV" stands at Wolverhampton Low Level, with strengthening coaches, to take over the 11.40am Birkenhead-Paddington at Wolverhampton Low Level, Whit Monday, 11th June 1962, in the last summer of steam for this line.   *(Michael Mensing)*

Castle No.5084 "Reading Abbey" passes Widney Manor with the up "Cambrian Coast Express", 18th April 1959.   *(Michael Mensing)*

For a main line

5022 "Wigmore Castle" hurries through Handsworth & Smethwick with a Birkenhead-Paddington express, 1st June 1957.

(John Edgington)

2-6-2T No.5192 on an afternoon Wolverhampton-Snow Hill stopping train at Bilston Central, 1st June 1957, as the down platform buildings were being renovated. Dmus were introduced on the route later that month. The present day Bilston Central Metro station is situated in the cutting, visible beyond the roof of the third carriage.

(John Edgington)

On 6th March 1967 Snow Hill awoke to an hourly service to Low Level, a shuttle to Langley Green which provided a connection with the Stourbridge line, and a few peak hour trains through the tunnel for the Stratford and Leamington lines. When I visited the station later that week, via what had become the only entrance in Great Charles Street, the building was still intact but bleak. Access to the main line platforms was denied by wooden boarding. The signs were all there, those showing where each car of the Blue Pullman once stopped creaked in the breeze. The public address system was still functioning, unused but switched on by mistake. The indistinct conversation of the booking office staff echoed along the platforms like the whispers of ghosts.

A first total closure proposal was unsuccessful, as a significant number of people still used the service and hardship would result. It was agreed that Dunstall Park station, west of Low Level on the former main line to Shrewsbury, could close, along with Snow Hill tunnel, on condition that the tunnel was retained for possible future use. These closures, in May 1968, also saw a reduction in the number of trains between Snow Hill and Low Level. The following year all stations lost their staff and the guard issued tickets on what were then known as 'pay trains'. The line received no publicity and no promotion. Passengers at Snow Hill had to use a sordid little side entrance in Livery Street. The bubble cars cowered within the weed infested wreck of a station, Platform 4 for Low Level, Platform 3 for Langley Green. Wolverhampton Low Level passengers entered their station via a squalid subway from High Level. Even as the trains continued to run, demolition of the vandalised buildings at intermediate stations began early in 1971. Given the deliberate slow throttling of this line, it is hardly surprising that passenger numbers declined and a second closure proposal was successful. The last train ran on the evening of Saturday 4th March 1972, a special hauled by a Class 47 loco, No.D1543. It ran to Stourbridge Junction and then back to New Street, probably the only through train ever to have run between Birmingham's two main stations.

Closure of the old Snow Hill marked the end of a historic station and, although not realised at the time, the end of passenger closures in the West Midlands for the remainder of the century. From the standpoint of 1972 it did not seem possible that some lines closed by Beeching could reopen and flourish, sixteen stations would be added to the West Midlands network and the single track three-times-a-day Redditch branch was to be electrified. Steam had a healthy future on and off the main line, privatised freight would grow again with or without the doctor's liner trains, passengers could travel once more between Snow Hill and London in under two hours, and between Snow Hill and Wolverhampton every six minutes. None of this could happen - could it?

Almost the end of the line. Not long before total closure in 1972, a single unit 'bubble car' dmu waits at Snow Hill's Platform 3 with a service for Langley Green. The sad little train, with no passengers in sight, is dwarfed by the huge bulk of the decaying station.

(Alan Searle)

ACKNOWLEDGEMENTS

Many people have readily offered help, advice, assistance, use of facilities, photographs, etc. in the preparation of this book. Particular thanks are due to the following -

Anna Burke   -   Birmingham Post librarian
Ray Churchill   -   railwayman
Michael Denholm   -   archive material
David Jopling   -   railwayman
Jim Male   -   railwayman
Simon Mole   -   Railtrack, Birmingham
Maurice Newman   -   railwayman
Robert Pearson   -   archive material
Horace Plant   -   railwayman
Don Powell   -   signalling information and archive material
Jane Rogers   -   GEC Alstholm, Metro-Cammell
Ken Werrett   -   proof reading

Some of the above provided photographs, as did the following -
Rodney Blanthorn, Roger Carpenter, Paul Catchpole, Robert Darlaston, John Edgington, Hugh Davies, Martin Davies, R.K.Blencowe, Michael Mensing, Peter Myatt, Jim Peden, Alan Searle, Roger Shenton, F.W.Shuttleworth, Ken Wort.

The author wishes to state that although he received much valuable assistance from railway staff and others working in an official capacity, any unattributable opinions expressed in the text of this book are entirely his own.

BIBLIOGRAPHY

BRITISH RAILWAYS 1948-73,
A Business History
T.R.Gourvish : Cambridge University Press : 1986 : ISBN 0 521 26480 4

THE HARBORNE EXPRESS
Smith & Harrison : Brewin Books : 1995 : ISBN 1 85858 045 5

THE LAST YEARS OF BRITISH RAILWAYS STEAM
O.S.Nock : David & Charles : 1978 : ISBN 0 7153 7583 0

NEW STREET REMEMBERED
Donald J.Smith : Barbryn Press : 1984 : ISBN 0 906160 05 7

PAST AND PRESENT, THE WEST MIDLANDS
John Whitehouse & Geoff Dowling : Past & Present Publishing : 1994 : ISBN 1 85895 075 9

A PICTORIAL RECORD OF BRITISH RAILWAYS DIESEL MULTIPLE UNITS
Brian Golding : Cheona Publications : 1995
ISBN 1 900 298 00 7

BIRMINGHAM RAILWAY CARRIAGE & WAGON CO.
Hypher & Wheeler : Runpast :1995 : ISBN 1 870754 34 4

A REGIONAL HISTORY OF THE RAILWAYS OF GREAT BRITAIN
Volume 7, The West Midlands
Rex Christiansen : David & Charles : 1973 : ISBN 07153 6093 0

RAIL CENTRES; WOLVERHAMPTON
Paul Collins : Ian Allan Ltd. : 1990 : ISBN 0 7110 1892 8

RAILWAYS OF THE WEST MIDLANDS, A CHRONOLOGY, 1808-1954
Ed. Charles Clinker : Stephenson Locomotive Society : 1954

SALUTE TO SNOW HILL
Derek Harrison : Barbryn Press : 1978 : ISBN 0 906 160 006

THE STORY OF NEW STREET
F.W.Grocott : published by British Railways London Midland Region to commemorate the centenary of the station, 1954.

Various journals, newspapers and documents, all acknowledged within the text.

Don't go without me. A peak hour steam working waits at Knowle & Dorridge to return to Moor Street with the 6.25pm train, 14th August 1959.
(Michael Mensing)

STATION GAZETTEER 1900-1972

This gazetter includes the names of stations, opening and closure dates to passenger traffic, other names, etc. Two sets of dates indicate opening, closure and re-opening (eg; Stourbridge Town), sometimes followed by final closure (eg; Princes End). Where no closure date is given, the station has been continuously open to passengers on the same or a similar site. Stations opened on new sites since 1972 (eg; Tame Bridge Parkway) are not listed.

ACOCKS GREEN 1852 (renamed 'Acocks Green & South Yardley' in 1878, now 'Acocks Green' again)
ADDERLEY PARK 1860
ALBION 1853-1960
ALDRIDGE 1879-1965
ALVECHURCH 1859
ASTON 1854
BAPTIST END 1905-1964
BARNT GREEN 1840
BERKSWELL 1844 (opened as Docker's Lane, renamed Berkswell 1853, Berkswell & Balsall Common 1882, now reverted to Berkswell.)
BESCOT 1847 (now 'Bescot Stadium')
BILSTON CENTRAL 1854-1972 ('Central' added in 1950)
BILSTON WEST 1854-1962 ('West' added in 1950)
BIRCHILLS 1858-1916
BIRMINGHAM MOOR ST. 1909-1987 (replaced by present stn. in 1987)
BIRMINGHAM NEW ST. 1851 (temporary stn.for local service to Wolverhampton) 1854 (main stn.)
BIRMINGHAM SNOW HILL 1852-1972 : 1987 ('Snow Hill' not added until 1858)
BLACKWELL 1840-1965
BLAKEDOWN 1852 (formerly CHURCHILL, then CHURCHILL & BLAKEDOWN)
BLAKE ST. 1884
BLOWERS GREEN 1878-1962 (named 'Dudley (South Side) & Netherton before 1921)
BLOXWICH 1858-1965 (new stn.to the north, 1989)
BORDESLEY 1855
BOURNVILLE 1876 (earlier known as STIRCHLEY ST. and STIRCHLEY ST.& BOURNVILLE)
BRADLEY & MOXLEY 1862-1915 (site near today's Bradley Lane Metro stop)
BRETTELL LANE 1852-1962
BRIERLEY HILL 1858-1962
BRIGHTON ROAD 1875-1941
BRINDLEY HEATH 1939-1959
BROCKMOOR HALT 1925-1932
BROMFORD BRIDGE 1896-1965 (racecourse stn., served only by specials)
BROMLEY HALT 1925-1932
BROMSGROVE 1840
BROWNHILLS (Midland) 1884-1930
BROWNHILLS (LNWR) 1849-1965
BUSHBURY 1852-1912
BUTLER'S LANE 1957-1991 : 1992 (new station on same site)
CAMP HILL 1841-1941
CANLEY 1940
CANNOCK 1859-1965 (new stn.1989)
CASTLE BROMWICH 1842-1968
CHESTER ROAD 1863
CHURCH ROAD 1876-1925
COLESHILL 1839-1916 remained open for goods and re-named MAXSTOKE IN 1923 (see also Forge Mills)
COMPTON HALT 1925-1932
COOMBES HOLLOWAY HALT 1905-1927
COSELEY 1902 (replaced Deepfields, opened 1852, 400 metres to north)
COVENTRY 1838
CRADLEY HEATH 1863 (earlier known as Cradley Heath & Cradley)
CUTNALL GREEN HALT 1928-1965
DAISY BANK 1854-1916 : 1919-1962
DANZEY 1908 (opened as Danzey for Tanworth)
DARBY END 1905-1964
DARLASTON 1837-1965 (known by various combinations of the words 'Darlaston' and 'James Bridge' until 1913, when the name was fixed by request of Darlaston Urban District Council)
DROITWICH 1852 (known as Droitwich Spa since 1923)
DUDLEY 1850-1964
DUDLEY PORT (Stour Valley platforms) 1852
DUDLEY PORT (South Staffordshire Line platforms) 1850-1964
DUNSTALL PARK 1896-1916 : 1919-1968
EARLSWOOD LAKES 1908 (now known as Earlswood)
ERDINGTON 1862
ETTINGSHALL ROAD 1852-1964
FIVE WAYS 1885-1944 : 1978
FOLESHILL 1850-1965
FORGE MILLS 1842-1965 (renamed COLESHILL in 1923)
FOUR OAKS 1884
GORNAL HALT 1925-1932
GRAVELLY HILL 1862
GREAT BARR 1862 (now named HAMSTEAD)

GREAT BRIDGE (NORTH) 1850-1964 ('North' added 1950)
GREAT BRIDGE (SOUTH) 1866-1915 : 1920-1964 ('South' added 1950)
GREAT WYRLEY 1858-1965 (also known as Wyrley & Cheslyn Hay)
GRIMES HILL & WYTHALL 1908 (opened as Grimes Hill Platform, now named WYTHALL)
HAGLEY opening date uncertain, first appeared in time-tables in 1862
HAGLEY ROAD 1874-1934
HALESOWEN 1878-1927 (open until 1960 for workmen's trains)
HALL GREEN 1908
HAMMERWICH 1849-1965
HAMPTON-IN-ARDEN (LNWR) 1837 (stn.moved 1/4 mile south-east to present site, 1884)
HAMPTON-IN-ARDEN (MR branch from Whitacre) 1839-1916
HANDSWORTH & SMETHWICK 1854-1972
HANDSWORTH WOOD 1896-1941
HARBORNE 1874-1934
HARTLEBURY 1852
HARTS HILL 1895-1916
HATTON 1852
HAZELWELL 1903-1941
HEATH TOWN 1872-1910
HEDNESFORD 1859-1965 : 1989
HENLEY-IN-ARDEN (branch terminus) 1894-1908
HENLEY-IN-ARDEN (North Warwickshire Line) 1908
HIMLEY 1925-1932
HOCKLEY 1854-1972 (site is west of the present Jewellery Quarter stn.)
HUNNINGTON 1883-1919 (stn.sidings served the Bluebird toffee factory)
ICKNIELD PORT ROAD 1874-1931
KENILWORTH 1844-1965
KIDDERMINSTER 1852
KINGSBURY 1839-1965
KINGS HEATH 1840-1941 (known as MOSELEY before 1867)
KINGS NORTON 1849
KNOWLE & DORRIDGE 1852 ('& Dorridge' added in 1899, now named just 'Dorridge')
LANDYWOOD 1908-1916 (new stn.1989)
LANGLEY GREEN 1885
LAPWORTH 1854 (known as KINGSWOOD until 1902)
LEA HALL 1939
LEAMINGTON SPA 1852 ('Spa' not added until 1913)
LEAMINGTON SPA AVENUE 1844-1965
LICHFIELD CITY 1849
LICHFIELD TRENT VALLEY 1847 (Trent Valley Line platforms)
LICHFIELD TRENT VALLEY 1849-1965 : 1988 (high level platforms)
LIFFORD 1885-1941 (third station)
LONGBRIDGE 1915-1960 (stn.on Halesowen branch, workmen's services only)
LYE 1863 (no station in Britain has a shorter name)
MARSTON GREEN 1844
MILVERTON 1844-1965 (opened as 'Leamington', underwent several name changes which included the words 'Warwick', 'Leamington' and 'Milverton' in various combinations)
MONMORE GREEN 1863-1916
MONUMENT LANE 1854-1958
MOSELEY 1867-1941
NEWTON ROAD 1837-1945
NORTHFIELD 1870
NORTH WALSALL 1872-1925
OCKER HILL 1864-1890 : 1895-1916
OLDBURY (LNWR main line) 1852 (replaced on same site by SANDWELL & DUDLEY in 1983)
OLDBURY (GWR branch terminus) 1885-1916
OLD HILL 1866
OLD HILL HIGH ST. HALT 1905-1964
OLTON 1869
PELSALL 1849-1965
PENN HALT 1925-1932
PENNS 1879-1965
PENSNETT HALT 1925-1932
PERRY BARR 1837 (the present station is on the same site as the Grand Junction Railway original)
PLECK 1881-1917 : 1924-1958
PRIESTFIELD 1854-1962 (Wolverhampton-Worcester line platforms)
PRIESTFIELD 1854-1972 (Wolverhampton-Birmingham line platforms)
Stn.site on curve, just south of Monmore Green stop on the Metro.

PRINCES END 1863-1890 : 1895-1916
PRINCES END & COSELEY 1853-1962 ('& Coseley' added in 1936)
REDDITCH 1859 (current stn. is fourth; second stn. 1868-1974; third 1974-1993)
ROTTON PARK ROAD 1874-1934
ROUND OAK 1852-1962 (known as 'Brierley Hill & Round Oak' before 1857)
ROWLEY REGIS 1867
RUBERY 1883-1919
RUGELEY TRENT VALLEY 1847
RUGELEY TOWN 1870-1965 : 1997
RUSHALL 1849-1909
SALTLEY 1854-1968
SELLY OAK 1876
SHENSTONE 1884
SHIRLEY 1908
SHORT HEATH (Clark's Lane) 1872-1931
SMALL HEATH 1863 (opened as 'Small Heath & Sparkbrook')
SMETHWICK 1852 (now named Smethwick Rolfe St.)
SMETHWICK JUNCTION 1867-1996 (later known as Smethwick West)
SOLIHULL 1852
SOHO (LNWR) 1867-1949
SOHO (GWR) 1854-1972 (known as Soho & Winson Green from 1893)
SOHO ROAD 1889-1941
SOMERSET ROAD 1876-1930
SPON LANE 1852-1960
SPRING ROAD 1908 (opened as Spring Road Platform)
STECHFORD 1844 (replaced by stn. on present site in 1882)
STOKE WORKS 1852-1965
STOURBRIDGE JUNCTION 1852 (present station and junction, south of earlier, opened 1901)
STOURBRIDGE TOWN 1879-1915 : 1919
STREETLY 1879-1965
SUTTON COLDFIELD 1862
SUTTON PARK 1879-1965
SUTTON TOWN 1879-1924
SWAN VILLAGE 1854-1972
TETTENHALL 1925-1932
THE HAWTHORNS 1931-1968 (served only by football specials)
THE LAKES 1935 (opened as The Lakes Halt)
TILE HILL 1864
TIPTON FIVE WAYS 1853-1962 ('Five Ways' added in 1950)
TIPTON OWEN ST. 1852 ('Owen St.' added, 1950-62)
TYSELEY 1906
VAUXHALL 1869 (also known as VAUXHALL & DUDDESTON, now known as DUDDESTON)
WALSALL 1847
WALSALL WOOD 1884-1930
WARWICK 1852
WATER ORTON 1842
WEDNESBURY CENTRAL 1854-1972 ('Central' added in 1950)
WEDNESBURY TOWN 1850-1964 ('Town' added in 1950)
WEDNESFIELD 1872-1931
WEST BROMWICH 1854-1972
WHITACRE 1842-1968 (stn. on junction site after 1864)
WHITLOCK'S END 1936 (opened as Whitlock's End Halt)
WIDNEY MANOR 1899
WILLENHALL 1837-1965
WILLENHALL STAFFORD ST. 1872-1931
WINDMILL END 1878-1964
WINSON GREEN 1876-1957
WITTON 1876
WOLVERHAMPTON HIGH LEVEL 1852 (known as 'Wolverhampton' 1852-1853 and since 1972; 'Wolverhampton Queen St.' 1853-1885 and 'Wolverhampton High Level' 1885-1972)
WOLVERHAMPTON LOW LEVEL 1854-1972 ('Low Level' added in 1856)
WOMBOURN 1925-1932
WOOD END 1908
WOOD GREEN 1881-1941 (also known as Wood Green [Old Bescot])
WYLDE GREEN 1862
YARDLEY WOOD 1908 (opened as Yardley Wood Platform)